Celebrate the Words and Experiences of Hope

Two Faces of Love

a memoir

Linda Lambert Pestana

with Anastra L. Madden

Here are touches of wisdom that come from Linda's heart ...

Two Faces of Love

a memoir

"At a young age, I learned not to judge an experience or an event simply by what I had seen, because so often it was not reality."

"My mother believed in God's mercy and because of her, I believed I should trust God, too."

"We don't go through loss, pain and emptiness and say they're blessings; however, I could say these events blessed my life because as a result of them, I became a different person."

"All that I lived in community helped to mold, fashion, and cultivate God's presence in my being, for which I will always be grateful."

"Left unchecked, fear had a power that robbed me not only of the moment but of my entire life."

Trust your heart and listen gently. I would love to hear from you. You can reach me by writing to Linda Pestana, P.O. Box 247, Norton, MA 02766, by email at twofacesoflove@aol.com or through my website at www.twofacesoflove.com.

Read what other people are saying about *Two Faces of Love...*

"I was going to read a few pages to get the gist of the story, and then come back to it later. Wrong! Over the years, I've seen in action parts of what has become Linda's story. She has been able to put the pieces together into a beautiful tapestry of love lived fully, a blending of struggle and joy!"

— Rev. George Bergin, svd

"This book, like its author, is 100% authentic. None of life's experiences is denied or withheld. Expect to be inspired to live your life to the fullest and to be exactly who you are. This is heartwarming, hopeful reading."

— Joan Hornsby, Ph.D.,
Clinical Psychologist

"I cried when she cried and laughed when she laughed. She displays our inner human dialogue in a way that will help readers understand that they are not alone. There are two lessons Linda shares that are essential for finding who you are. First, find your unique and authentic talent; and second, learn how to pick up pain, embrace it, and dance with it. We need to do all of this in order to grow. Anyone interested in personal development should use *Two Faces of Love* as a road map."

— Celeste M. Warner
President, CMW, Training & Development

Annedawn Publishing
Box 247, Norton, MA 02766
800-985-7878
annedawn@aol.com
http://www.twofacesoflove.com

Copyright © 2000 by Annedawn Publishing. All rights reserved.
First Printing 2000
Printed in the United States of America
Designed by Don Langevin

Library of Congress Cataloging in Publication Data
Pestana, Linda Lambert
Servant, Christopher, editor

Two Faces of Love / Linda Lambert Pestana
1st edition.
Library of Congress Catalog Card Number: 99-97679

ISBN 0-9632793-9-4

10 9 8 7 6 5 4 3 2 1

DEDICATION

...to my Mother for blessing me with life,
the power of love,
and the greatest gift of all,
my faith.

...to my husband Louis for sharing my life,
his tender love, gentleness,
and total support of my dreams.

CONTENTS

ACKNOWLEDGEMENTS

Writing my memoir was a challenging, lengthy process that could not have been accomplished without the support, guidance, and dedication from a woman whom I have come to call friend, Anastra Madden. Anastra found the voice to my thoughts and feelings, and carried the underlying thread of my story onto the written page. She was my writer, therapist, and companion who forever called me to go deeper within myself. She challenged me to speak my own truth that, over time, called me home to the essential Linda.

I am thankful to Don Langevin — a real angel. My life has been blessed by his support and skill at editing, along with a multitude of talents, which have been invaluable in helping to make this book, my story, a reality. I also offer special appreciation to Marge Guimond for introducing us to our publisher, Annedawn Publishing.

I am thankful to Mary-Lou Mancini, Deanna Mello, Kathy Murphy, Patricia McGowan, and Claudette Martelly for providing invaluable feedback and suggestions as the manuscript evolved to its present form. I also want to thank my friend Leon Gonsalves for his unending support.

There are many whose lives touched mine and helped my story come to birth. My spiritual director, Peggy Perring Mulligan, was the first person to lovingly challenge me to write my story, along with my sister and dear friend, Cora Thompson. I am particularly grateful to Janet Gagnon, Lewella Daigle, and my sister, Judy Carr, for their insights and reflections that were significant to this work.

I am grateful that my life has been blessed with friends whose support and love taught me so much: Fred and Carmen Pestana, Dr. Richard Hellwig, Madeleine Deschenes, and James Willsey.

I give thanks for my family and the support that set the stage for who I am today. They are my sisters Carol, Claire, Judy, Cora, my brother Charles, and in loving memory of my brother, Bobby. They were and continue to be an inspiration to me. I honor and cherish each one.

I am grateful to a great many people whose names do not appear on this page, but their love, friendship, and support are forever written into my heart.

I especially wish to acknowledge the unflinching support, encouragement, and love of my husband and best friend, Louis. His sense of humor and perspective were invaluable during the lengthy process of writing my story. I could not have done it without him.

For her love and acceptance, a special thanks must also go to our daughter, Jennifer. Above all, I give gratitude to God.

My Husband and Best Friend
Lou Pestana

PREFACE

Sharing my story was a journey inward into my own heart. It was not an easy experience for me to do. I had to revisit unwanted emotions and difficult situations that I preferred to avoid. I felt I walked naked on these pages, exposing the shameful feelings and memories of the past; but I was convinced that if I could remain faithful, honest, and vulnerable with my story, perhaps others could draw comfort, courage, and strength, thus seeing something of their own lives reflected in mine.

The gift of this effort was that by allowing myself to recall pleasant and painful memories, the experience of healing and wholeness gradually unfolded for me. I am amazed at how different I am today than when I first began this journey.

I hope and pray that as you, dear reader, move deeper into your own journey, you will gain greater clarity and a stronger sense of your own vitality of soul. May you awaken to the beauty in yourself, in others, and in life.

— Linda Lambert Pestana, October, 1997

PART ONE
FIRST ROOTS

Throughout our lifetime there are many entry points

which lead us to new levels of reality.

Life sometimes asks us to go where it hurts,

to enter into broken places of pain, fear, and confusion.

Working with those areas that block and hinder growth,

making the unconscious conscious,

and going through the center of suffering,

is that journey which truly brings one

to letting go and letting be what is.

∞

ONE
THE BEGINNING

I was born but not wanted. I was loved but never felt lovable. I was good, kind, and loving, but never felt good enough, kind enough or loving enough. Never did my mother express these thoughts to me, but I believe I was born with the scars of these thoughts. I know my mother loved me. I know she wanted me, but sometimes life can squeeze all that loving and wanting out of us. No one is to blame. It's just the way things were back then.

I was born the fifth child, having an older brother and three older sisters. Early memories, and events my family lived through before my appearance, belong to my mother, older siblings, relatives, and town records. I wanted to understand the setting I was born into because I arrived at a time when years of tension, marital discord, and overwhelming hardship had repeatedly punctuated my family's life. Recollections from others painted the bigger picture that eventually fed into who I thought I was and how I came to live it.

My father's family moved to South Berwick, Maine, my mother's home town, during the Depression in the late 1920s. My father, William Lambert, was twenty years old. The Lambert family had come from Fall River, Massachusetts where they had lost their farm, their home, their furniture, everything. They stayed with relatives in nearby Somerset, Massachusetts, but they, like everyone else at the time, were barely able to make it. My grandfather, Edward Lambert, heard there were some opportunities further north in South Berwick, and he managed to move the family there. They ended up staying.

A bird's eye view of South Berwick shows a small triangular tract of land about 31.6 square miles near the southern tip of Maine. It is framed to the north by the towns of Berwick and North Berwick, and to the east by the coastal resort town of Wells. Elliot and York communities shore up the south end before reaching the Atlantic. The Salmon Falls and Piscataqua Rivers complete its borders on the west. Nestled within its boundaries are four ponds: Knight's, Cox's, Warren's, and Round. There are a total of twenty-three bridges, many of which suture the town with its southern New Hampshire neighbors. The late nineteenth century had been a prosperous time for South Berwick, especially with the boom of the shoe industry which gave rise to other related businesses. When my father and his family moved there, the town, though financially hard pressed, had several mills, shoe shops, tanneries, other small businesses, and farming opportunities. By then, the town was famous as the home of author Sarah Orne Jewett and the prestigious Berwick Academy.

Despite its relatively small size, South Berwick had a number of churches of different denominations whose steeples rose above with the classic three-storied New England homes, industrial housing projects, and some outlying farm houses. Among these, and centered in town, was St. Michael's Roman Catholic Church. In 1909, the Sisters of St. Joseph took charge of St. Michael's parochial school where my mother and all of us children attended until the eighth grade. They also established a convent and St. Joseph's Academy, an all girls' high school. The Catholic Church, with its religious culture and rigid mores, had for years blended with the town's Yankee mentality. Everything was either black or white, right or wrong. There was no heart for all the gray areas of life's hardships. There would come a time when the Church would play a significant, and at times, painful role in my mother's life.

My mother, Helen Marie St. Laurent, had remarkable resiliency. It was a certain kind of buoyancy, a lightness, that was grounded in a bare bones faith. Catholicism was the outer covering, but the nuts and bolts of her faith were her own. She lived out of that faith. She loved to celebrate life and to accommodate others. She was a very warm person and would never hesitate to welcome others or set another place at the table. There was also a part of her that would look the other way when things got too painful. She was always concerned about what other people would think. "Whatever happens at home, remains at home," was echoed to us many times while growing up. Her coping mechanisms made her a survivor. They were her gift and her nemesis, tightly wrapped into one package.

When I think about it, it may have been my mother's lightness and joy in the small things that first attracted my father to her. He was a gregarious sort of person, extremely personable and sociable. He had a gift of gab, and could and would talk to anyone. His friends considered him the life of the party. He went out of his way to be generous and helped anyone who needed it. People loved him. When my mother married him in the summer of 1936, she didn't know that he wasn't always like that. She didn't know his generosity was only reserved for others. At home, it was a different story.

My mother was twenty and my father was twenty-six when they married. The first two years before the children came along, according to her, were good. My mother worked in a shoe factory and my father was self-employed as a molder. He had his own shop making concrete cement blocks. My father's family loved his new wife, and they remained in touch with her even after he was no longer in the picture. My mother's parents, however, felt differently about their son-in-law. There was something about him that they didn't like, and they tried to discourage my mother from marrying him. Dad had an abusive streak in him, and after they were married, he would sometimes slap my mother. Even my father's family tried to protect her. On one occasion my father's sister-in-law was present during one of their arguments. Irene could tell that he was getting ready to hit my mother. She stepped between them, thinking she wouldn't get hit, but she did. That's the way he was.

Soon after they were married, my father decided to build a home with both my parents working on it. It was not fancy, but my mother was thrilled to have her own place. She did a lot of the work whenever she could, and her hands really showed the wear and tear of her efforts. Her mother-in-law was worried, but my mother told her, "My hands will heal, but at least I'll have a home." After they finished the house, my father decided to give it to his parents because they didn't have a place of their own. My mother was left out of the decision. That's how things happened with them.

In April of 1938, my oldest brother, Robert, was born, but we always called him Bobby. After his birth, things gradually began to change. My father moved the family out into the country. As they started having more babies, my father embarked upon one business venture after another. His persuasive personality allowed him to sell to just about anyone. He also could talk anyone into lending him money, which often got him into trouble and, at one time, even landed him in jail. He didn't have a problem getting money, but he did have a problem repaying his creditors. He often had big plans for making himself rich, but his ventures always failed.

My sisters, Carol, Claire, and Judy were each born a few years apart, and in between some of those years, my mother miscarried twice. During that time, my father built another home, still out in the country. This time he did much of the work himself. It wasn't elaborate by any means. In time, however, creditors knocked on the door and demanded payment for past due bills. My mom was beside herself; she knew nothing about it because my dad kept her in the dark about finances most of the time. They eventually lost the house, but that didn't stop him. He built another one and that, too, was lost shortly after I was born. Owned or rented, the homes were always in the country away from town. With no car, no money, and all those babies, my mother couldn't go anywhere. Whenever she could get a ride, she would attend Sunday mass at St. Michael's which meant a lot to her. Years later, I remember her saying that my father wanted to keep her "barefoot and pregnant," and he did. While she was taking care of the kids, he was off on another scheme to make himself rich. Women had little say in those days.

My sister Judy was just fifteen months old at the time of my birth. Marital problems had been brewing for a number of years, and my father's abuse had escalated. Worries about where money for food and other basic essentials would come from left my mom fearful and dependent. She handled it by praying a lot. She believed in God, simply and profoundly. Her faith and love for her children kept her going through the isolation of the country and chronic financial hardship. Her faith even accommodated a negligent husband who was never there for her, and now there would be another mouth to feed, mine.

As the delivery date approached, my father spent more and more time away from home. The situation was more than grim, so it didn't surprise me to learn that on October 29, 1948, I came out feet first. The breech birth caused a lot of tearing in my mother's body and trauma to me. Sickly for several months with intestinal problems, I couldn't keep milk down and required special formula. While in the hospital, my mother was in a room with four other women who had also given birth. One day the nurse came in wanting to know whose husband William Lambert was. My mother said, "That's my husband and Linda is my child." The woman lying in the bed next to her said, "William Lambert is also the father of my son." That's how my mother found out that my father was cheating on her. When she came home, a hospital bill for the other baby had already arrived in the mail.

The internal conflict for my mother was immense. She was trapped in a small country home on Knight's Pond Road with four older children and a new baby. Years of emotional and physical abuse plus financial dependency had taken their toll. Most of all, she feared what other people would think. She dreaded the religious and social stigma attached to a divorced woman. It was the climate of the times, and she was a devout Catholic. The Church's position on divorce was clear; it was not an option. As interpreted, it was not only a grievous sin, but in those days the "sinner" was threatened with excommunication and banished from all church functions and services. In 1948, divorced Catholics were not entitled to receive the sacraments, not allowed a Catholic funeral Mass, or to be buried in a Catholic cemetery. For my mother, there didn't seem to be much choice but to stay married and hold the family together.

Several months after I was born, we lost the third house my father had built. The house was in foreclosure, and we were evicted in the middle of winter. My father, who was still at home, uprooted the family one more time and moved us out of South Berwick to a small cottage in Wells Beach, Maine. During this time, my father was less available than ever. I think we were a constant reminder of how he had failed to provide for his wife and children. He readily gave money to the poor, but he had trouble feeding his own family. All his dreams, and big ideas to become rich, had been only mirages in a desert where there were no respite from the withering heat of the sun. For my mother, this move to Wells was pivotal.

In the winter, Wells Beach was a dreary, desolate place. A howling wind coming off of the ocean replaced the summer breeze and bustle of tourists. Thick, gray clouds cast a bleak spell over everything. Removed by distance for the first time from family, friends, Church, and familiar surroundings, the isolation for my mother became unbearable. It was cold. There was no money and very little food. She didn't know how she could feed and care for all of us on her own. She was desperate. She was a young woman with five children, she was in a very fragile state of mind, and everyone sensed that she was ready to give up. One night she planned to kill all of us, and then kill herself, thinking this was the best way to get out of the pain and nightmare we were in.

The next morning, when she got up, something had changed. It was as if she awoke from a bad dream, and said to herself, "My God, I need help. I can't do that!" She had five children she loved and who needed her. She couldn't go through with it, and couldn't believe she had seriously considered ending all our lives. It was an option she never returned to, but she knew she had to do something. There was little heat, hardly any food left, and she had no idea when my father would return. She thought we would all die if we stayed there. She needed to get us back to South Berwick, and she knew she had to make a choice and leave him. With help from family and friends, my mother took us back to South Berwick and she followed through in divorcing my father. The needs of her children took priority over the condemnation of the Church and the community.

My mother was not perfect, but she had courage, courage rooted in her faith and her belief in God. That was the core of her strength, her tenacity, and her ability to stand firm in the face of intense opposition. It's a good thing. She was going to need it.

Whenever she could, she quietly attended church and brought the older children with her. One particular Sunday morning she was sitting among other parishioners while my brother and sisters sat in the front rows with their classmates. The church pews were filled and the service proceeded as usual until it came time for the homily. The pastor walked across the sanctuary and slowly climbed into the pulpit. People waited as he looked over the congregation, and when he found whom he was looking for, his whole expression changed. His face flushed as he glared at my mother. You could hear a pin drop. The pastor raised his arm and pointed his finger directly at my mother. "You don't belong here!" he screamed. "You're a divorced woman. In the eyes of the Church, you are living in mortal sin! You are excommunicated, and you are not part of this congregation anymore. You are no longer welcome here." There was a stunned silence; he paused and then he added, "I want you to leave now!" My mother grabbed her purse and hurriedly left the church looking at the floor in front of her all the way out. She stopped going to church after that.

My mother never expressed anger toward the Church or the pastor. She rarely spoke of the incident, but when she did, her eyes filled up and her voice quivered. "It was a terrible experience," she'd say, "it was so humiliating." That's all she offered. My mother later learned that the pastor had taken my brother and older sister out of class to talk with them about her. No one seems to remember exactly what he said, but it prompted my mom to pull my siblings out of St. Michael's and transfer them to public school. They stayed there only a short time before they begged her to return to St. Michael's to be with their friends. She let them.

As I grew up, I remember thinking how my mother was the most wonderful person in the world. I thought she could do no wrong and, even at a young age, I was very protective of her. With our young Catholic minds, my siblings and I canonized her. We knew her as a bouncy, lighthearted person who did much with little to bring joy into our lives. She had a way of celebrating life that was contagious, and it bound us to her. We knew her as a woman who loved and cared for us despite extreme hardships. She was a woman of indomitable faith in God which she passed on to us in her words and in the way she lived. Her faith grew even more as time went on, and this played an important part in the life of my family. These were her strengths, and we lived them through her until they became our own.

I have no memory of my father or of the events that led to the divorce. Personal recollections of my past would not surface for another few years when my stepfather was with us. My mother met Bob shortly after her divorce through mutual friends, and they were married within a year. Both shared a mutual dependence on the other and, for my mother, there was a viable hope for stability. Although he earned only a modest living as an oil truck driver, Bob could hold down a job. This was Bob's first marriage, and at first he was kind to her and to us. I think my mother couldn't believe he was willing to marry a divorced woman with five children. She did believe, however, that his drinking was really nothing to worry about.

At first, it wasn't.

TWO
THE FARM

I was about two years old when Bob joined our family. We moved into his small country farmhouse outside of town. There was lots of land, a large barn, animals and beautiful pines out back. Part of me carries warm memories of popcorn parties, birthday celebrations, and times of just celebrating life with one another. My mother would gather us together and call it our "night on the town." We'd sing, share stories, tell jokes, play games, and laugh together. Another part of me holds memories I'd prefer to forget. They hurt going in, and they seem to hurt more when they came out years later. This was the home that taught me that life is a mysterious combination of laughter and pain, of joy and sorrow, of things good and bad. We just didn't have any idea how bad it was going to get.

The farmhouse was a very simple two-story home with a tin roof that made a wonderful sound when it rained. There was a small foyer at the entrance where my mom had lined up our own hooks so we could hang our jackets. To the left of the foyer there was a medium-sized kitchen that was painted yellow. It had a wood stove, a table and chairs. Attached to it was a small pantry. My mother had the wood stove going nearly all the time, and we loved the aromas of her cooking that permeated the house. The wood stove was also the only source of heat in the house. Adjacent to the kitchen was a living room painted purple with a simple couch, chairs and end tables. There was a piano which, every so often my mother played, and we thought she was wonderful. Off the living room was a small bedroom where my mother and stepfather slept. Next to the entrance of their room were narrow wooden stairs that led up to the second floor where the five of us slept. Later, there would be seven of us until my brother, Bobby, left home at age 18. The upstairs had two unfinished bedrooms, a larger one and a smaller one, with a tiny closet in between. The closet was made of thin slats through which we could see into each

11

other's room. There was no finished ceiling. Everything was open, exposing the sturdy beams supporting the roof.

We were very poor, but I never realized it. It never occurred to me that we had less than others because my mother allowed us to experience life. She had a way of lifting us, of making a game out of very simple things. We didn't have running water in the house, no electricity, and no toilet. We used the outhouse by the side of the woodshed. About a year before we left the farm, we did have electricity installed and a television set and radio, which we thought was pretty exciting. We didn't have a regular bathtub, so my mother would bring in a huge water pail, heat some water, and fill it. She made sure the makeshift tub was near the wood stove to keep us warm. We'd take our turns bathing, and we were delighted. That was the thrill and anticipation of Saturday night, our Saturday night bath. We were happy with little things. Jump ropes, marbles, and coloring books were treasured possessions. We thought we had it all.

In the beginning my stepfather, Bob, was good to us. We always had food and shelter which was better than what we had before. During their first year together, my mother became pregnant with my sister, Cora. During the pregnancy, Bob's mother died. My stepfather took his mother's death hard. Bob was very close to his mother, and he never recovered from losing her. That's when things began to change at home.

Bob became either very sad and quiet or angry and mean, especially when he drank. He seemed to drown his grief, and from day to day, especially on weekends, we never knew what kind of mood he would be in. He still took care of us and provided for us, but it was different. When Cora was born, he liked the idea of naming her after his mother, but he was disappointed that he didn't have a son. He blamed my mother for not giving him a boy and made life miserable for her. He became verbally abusive to her and then the beatings started. He was also abusive to my older siblings, but because we were little, he left Cora and me alone. I had the feeling he liked me because he would smile at me, or bounce me on his knee. But, I had a hard time accepting him because I was always scared for my mother and older brother and sisters. I didn't want them to get hurt.

Family life was mixed. We had fun when he wasn't there. When he was, and he had been drinking, there was a lot of tension. He was very mean when he drank. I remember once waking up in the middle of the night and hearing a commotion downstairs. I ran down in time to see him beating my mother and throwing her from one side of the room to the other. She had a bloody nose and one eye that was all swollen. I ran up to her, wrapped myself around her leg and screamed, "Daddy, don't hurt her! Don't hurt her!" That was my first conscious memory of trying to protect her. I was five years old.

We all went to St. Michael's parochial school. I loved school and enjoyed learning. I had good friends, and I especially loved the Sisters of St. Joseph. They took an interest in me, they were warm, and they laughed easily. If I talked about home at school, it was always about how much we loved each other and how much fun we had as a family. Most of that was true, but I didn't talk about the tension and fear.

I don't know how I knew, but I always knew that divorce was not acceptable in our community. I wanted to defend my mother, but I was also ashamed that she was divorced. So I told my friends that my father died and my mother had remarried. The people in South Berwick who went to St. Michael's came from Franco-American backgrounds, and these families were closely knit. Your family problem was your problem, and it didn't go any place else, yet, people were still quick to judge. That was always very difficult for me. I was sensitive to how people felt and how they thought. I wanted them to know the correct story, but feared rejection from my friends. I learned to hide everything inside.

I dreaded weekends because that meant that my stepfather was around, and he would be drinking. The dread was for my mother and my older siblings, especially for Bobby. My stepfather was awful to him, and it really left a mark on Bobby. I don't know why, but Bobby was deathly afraid of chickens. My stepfather knew this. He would go and grab one of the chickens from the chicken coop and he would make Bobby cut the head off. Sometimes the head wasn't completely cut off and the chicken would start running around. My stepfather would get hold of that bloody chicken and run after Bobby with it. Bobby would scream and cry, and try to get away.

When my stepfather was at work, I thought I was the happiest child in the world. I had my family, and that's what mattered to me. I was able to separate the bad from the good. Without consciously knowing it, I learned to cope by being the family clown. Whatever it took to make people laugh, I would do it. I always knew when to do it, and when to break the tension. I picked up on people's feelings, and when those feelings turned ugly or fearful, I would do something. I'd bump into things, do some kind of crazy acrobatic move, tell a joke and forget the punch line, or just start singing. Everyone would laugh and the tension would fizzle. I wasn't aware of what I was doing, but I know I lived out of that place inside where I separated bad from good. At the time, I felt it was my mission in life to make people feel better about themselves by making them laugh at me. This pattern lasted well into my adult life.

We had animals on the farm, including a billy goat. I hated that goat, and that goat hated me. I think the goat knew I didn't like him, so whenever he got loose, he would chase me. He'd come after me with his little horns, and I'd run. That goat would chase me everywhere as I ran. We had a driveway which was about a quarter of a mile long, but it seemed longer. I would run all the way down it, get at the end, and then turn around because there was no other place to go. I'd run all the way back with the billy goat butting all the way. I'd cry and my sister, Judy, would stand there and laugh. Evidently, the goat and I made quite a picture. We also raised pigs, usually two at a time. We would get them nice and fat, and then they'd become our meat for the winter. I don't know how they did it, but one pig would always get loose and chase me. I swear I had something the animals detected that made them come after me.

On the farm, we played a lot as a family because we only had each other. There weren't a whole lot of people around. That really bonded us. Our playground was the open fields, the big barn out back, and the stand of pine trees in back of that. We loved to play games, one being hide and seek. I could never figure out why Judy, who was only a year older than I, always found me. One time I was determined she wasn't going to. There was a thick clump of woods near the side of the house that made a perfect hiding place. I climbed in there, sat on a tree stump, and waited for Judy to come by. I was wearing shorts that had a little clasp at the end of each leg

to make it snug around the thigh. It's a good thing I had those shorts on, because pretty soon there was a bunch of red ants crawling all over my legs and up my shirt. It was easy for Judy to find me; all she had to do was follow the screams. Another time, I decided to go where no one ever went, and I mean, no one. I decided to hide in the pigpen that was in our barn. Because of my size, the only way I could get in was to crawl on my belly through the feeder. It had a door with a hinge that swung shut. It turned out to be pretty snug, and I got caught in the feeder door. I couldn't move forward or backward and my legs were sticking out. I started yelling for someone to help me. Judy found me that time too.

We all helped with the farm chores, yet we played at doing them. My mother did a lot of the work like milking the cow and tending the large vegetable garden, but we all took turns taking care of the animals. Bobby and my mother would chop wood, and we all helped pile and stack it. After chores were done, we played jump rope, marbles, and roll the can, or we used our tree swing. There was also a large barrel that we got inside and rolled down the hill. In the winter, we didn't have enough sleds to go around so we would use cardboard to go sledding. We loved it, especially when my mom came out and joined us.

Christmas time was special because of my Aunt Hazel and Aunt Dot. They were my step-father's sister and aunt. If they had not been there, we would not have had a Christmas. They remained our Santa Claus even after my mother divorced Bob. They loved my mom, and they loved us. They filled our Christmas with special presents. A game, a doll, clothes, or sweet treats from them meant so much. My mother tried hard, but she had barely enough to feed us. She would do what she could, and what she gave us, we loved and treasured.

We always lived in "hand-me-downs." Judy would get Claire's clothes, I would get Judy's, and Cora would get mine. My mother made a lot of our clothes. When we started wearing petticoats, she'd starch them so they fanned out beautifully under our dresses. We thought we looked beautiful and elegant. When we did get a new dress, we could barely contain ourselves. Being poor never entered my mind. We were happy with each other and with whatever came our way. We were secure in our mother's love.

Everything was fine while my stepfather was away at work or out for the evening. On a night, when he came home drunk, it was terrible. I would panic when I heard the door close. I never knew what was going to happen to my mother. The abuse and the beatings didn't happen every night, but even one night was one too many. When Bob was drunk, he would often go to bed with a knife and gun under his pillow. My mother lived in fear. I never had a sense of a good, kind, and loving father. I always wanted one, sensed that it could be, but the only one I knew scared me. Whatever scared me, I blocked out of my mind.

When Cora was about two years old, my mother became pregnant with my youngest brother, Charlie. I remember she was huge, she was all baby. Our water came from an outdoor well where during the day the sun would beat down on it, and the snakes would come out and lay on the rocks. My mother was terrified of snakes. To this day, so am I. My stepfather thought he'd have fun and grabbed one of the snakes and chased my mother with it. She was so big she had trouble running. I'll never forget the horror, the fright on her face, and her screams. I ran up to my mother and hung on to her leg. I kept yelling at him, "Don't do that to her! Stop it! STOP IT!" My stepfather was mixed up. He felt powerful scaring people, beating them or saying vicious things to them. Without the bottle he was docile. We never knew what to expect, but always lived in fear. We all learned to survive, cope, and above all, not tell anyone what went on in our home.

When Charlie was about ten months old, my mother had to go into the hospital for a hysterectomy. While there, she got a severe staph infection and was a thread away from death. The doctors said she was not going to survive. My mom actually overheard them say, "This woman is all but dead." We later learned she made a promise to Mary, the Blessed Mother, that if she survived to raise her children, she would light three candles in church every Sunday in her name. Otherwise, she asked Mary to not prolong her life and to let her die. Mom was good at negotiating with our Blessed Mother and the saints, and she did pull through, but it took more than two months for her to recuperate. Until the end of her life, my mother kept her weekly promise to Mary.

My stepfather stayed clear of my mother while she was in the hospital. He couldn't cope with any kind of stress and rarely visited her. My oldest sisters, Carol and Claire, took care of the four of us during this time. Our meals were peanut butter and jelly sandwiches and canned chicken noodle soup. We ate it and didn't say a word, but to this day, I don't like canned chicken noodle soup.

When my mother came home she was weak, yet she continued working as hard as before. Because we were at school, she was the one who milked the cows, brought in the wood, and cooked and cleaned the house. She did whatever needed to be done, and in many ways, she was our jack of all trades. My stepfather didn't do anything to help. She often said, "Maybe if I sat back, it would be different." Mom did too much for the men in her life. She treated them too well and gave and gave until she didn't have anything left to give. They never gave back.

One summer day when I was about seven years old, a friend of my mother's came over to visit. They sat at the kitchen table and talked over a cup of coffee. I happened to be in the house at the time and overheard my mother say my name in conversation. I became instantly alert. My mother talked about my birth and how difficult the delivery was. "I really hadn't planned on another pregnancy," she said. "It was the wrong time. Things were so bad back then, the last thing I wanted was another baby." I stood in the other room frozen on the spot. I couldn't breath; I couldn't feel; I couldn't think; my brain went blank. Hurting her or losing her love was unimaginable. At that moment, something changed inside of my heart, and I decided right then and there that I would work real hard at being a good girl, a perfect little girl. I would be so good that she would no longer regret having had me. I ran outside to play. I was the clown again, and I felt much better.

Bobby had left home to get married. He was only 18. He thought he was in love, but I think he just wanted to get out of the house. He lived across the river in Somersworth, New Hampshire, about six miles from the farm. I loved Bobby and we all missed him. Bobby was a natural comedian. He had these unusual facial expressions that just made you laugh. Like my father, he was very sociable, but, like my stepfather, he later developed a drinking problem that lasted for a number of years. This was hard on everyone who loved him. Today, I know that if it weren't for Bobby, and my sisters Carol and Claire, I don't think my mother would have lived as long as she did. I know they helped her through a really horrible time.

Charlie, my youngest brother, was about three or four when everything seemed to fall apart. My mother changed. She wasn't bouncy or happy anymore. She became lethargic and very depressed. I didn't know, or didn't understand that she was having a nervous breakdown. I think my mother felt stuck in her situation and didn't know what to do. She started going downhill inside herself and things came to a crisis. It seemed as if my mom had given up and if someone didn't help her, she was going to die. That's what Bobby and my sisters saw in my mother. We had to either get her out, or something terrible was going to happen.

One day, when my stepfather was at work, Bobby and Carol came and took my mother and all of us away. We just left and didn't take anything with us. He took us to his home in Somersworth. That's when my mother finally decided to divorce my stepfather and got herself a lawyer. The lawyer advised her, "Because you left, whatever you want, you have to go back to get. If you're caught, it's going to have to be returned." That was a terrifying time. We were little; we didn't understand and didn't know what was going to happen. My mother and older siblings went back to the farm while my stepfather was at work. They quickly packed, loaded things, and made sure everything was out before he came home. It was a scary experience because if my stepfather had been drinking and caught my mother removing things, he would have beaten her.

Not long after that, I learned my stepfather wanted custody of Cora and Charlie. They were his children, but I think he also wanted to get back at my mother for leaving him. I was too young to know that they would stay with us. All along, I feared something might go wrong, and I couldn't bear the thought of losing my brother and sister. Cora and Charlie did stay with us, but until I was sure in my young mind that they would, I constantly worried about it.

We stayed in Bobby's home for a few weeks. It was the first time I had seen a shower and it frightened me. I was told, "Go in and take a shower." Well, I didn't know how it worked. I turned the water on, and I thought the whole shower head was going to fall on top of me. It was also the first time we had a flush toilet and I thought that was a wonderful invention. We stayed with Bobby for just a little while. My mother talked with some people and received help from the town of South Berwick, and then moved us back there. She found a second story apartment that was large enough for all of us.

Our life changed so much after this. The best thing about it was that my mother came back to life. She got her energy back, was interested in life, laughed easily, and worked just as hard as ever. She made many repairs in the apartment and we all were happy there. We could breathe without tension. My nerves, our nerves, could rest. We no longer had to worry when my stepfather would come home. We didn't have to wonder if he would come home drunk, or if he would be in a good or bad mood. Now that he was gone, we just enjoyed each other. From that point on, my mother was a single parent and raised us by herself.

Divorce in our life, and in the life of our community, spelled 'different.' The Church and parochial school preached without tolerance that family life was important and divorce was not acceptable. I often found myself trying to protect my family. People didn't understand. Judgments were made and Mom was often criticized. I often remember the struggle I had with my friends about having a brother and sister with a different last name. My friends would say to me, "They're not your real brother and sister, they're only your half brother and sister." I couldn't believe what I was hearing. I knew they were my family. They were not half "anything" to me or to anyone in my family. Judgments like that cut deep and left scars. I felt isolated and alone, even with my closest friends. After my mother divorced the second time, my birth father came back into our lives. For a nine year old, this was a big event, but I didn't know what to think about it. I felt confused and looked for cues from my mother who simply said, "Linda, this is your father. I will never stop him from seeing his children." He would come and was welcomed. We spoke to him, and heard him speak. We saw him, and he us, and there was some growth of a bonding love between father and child. Mom, aware of this, allowed my sisters and brother and me to get to know him even further.

My father was 5'7" tall and weighed about 200 pounds. He had brown eyes, black hair and always had a ready smile. He had a dimple in the middle of his chin just like my brother Bobby. I remember his brown baseball cap that he wore tilted to the side. People who knew my dad said I was the spitting image of him. He had remarried and was still living in South Berwick. Bobby, Carol and Claire had visited him from time to time, but Judy and I had never seen him until the year he decided to visit with us.

It took me a long time to trust this man and allow him into my life. He was my "father," but, what that meant exactly, I wasn't sure. Unlike my stepfather, his connection to me was of blood, and it had a different feel to it. I really didn't know who he was as a person or what our relationship should be because I was just a baby when my mother left him. I did know that I wanted to spend time with him.

I remember once he had Judy and me on his lap. He told us with tears in his eyes how sorry he was for all that he had put us through. "I realize," he said, "what I lost when your mom left me, and I would love to have her back, but it's too late." He took a deep breath and said again how sorry he was. Something in him touched my heart, and it was the first time I remember hugging him.

Judy and I both wanted more time with him. Instead, he would give us each 50 cents and tell us to go buy candy or an ice cream. At the time, two quarters was a lot of money, and we wanted that, but we also wanted to be bounced around on his knee and to be noticed. I think we didn't get a whole lot of attention because he didn't know how to relate to 9 and 10 year old children. The others were older and were able to talk the talk of grownups. He seemed more at ease with them, and I didn't want to break that ease, so I had only rare, childlike conversations with him. When he visited, I watched and remember how he told stories and cracked jokes. He also did his best to listen to the others because he wanted to make up for all the bad times he had put Mom and us through. He really felt sad for the things he had and hadn't done. The past couldn't be changed, but he tried by dividing his time between us and his other family, and that meant a lot to us. None of us knew how little time we had left with him.

∞

THREE
THE SOUTH BERWICK YEARS

The day was December 12, 1958 and I had turned ten at the end of October. My mother had asked me to stop by the grocery store to pick up some meat on my way home from school. While waiting for the meat cutter to make up my package, I overheard a conversation. Some of the grownups were talking about a William Lambert who had died. One man was saying, "Yeah, Lambert and his son were trucking logs from the woods and heading for the saw mill. They never made it. Lambert was driving, had a heart attack, and fell over the steering wheel. His son managed to stop the truck." The other man raised his cap, scratched his head, readjusted his cap, and said, "Well, that's a damn shame." It never occurred to me they were talking about my dad. I got the meat and headed for home. When I got there, Bobby and my older sisters were crying and having a real hard time. That's when I realized the William Lambert the men were talking about was my

father; the son was Bobby. I was old enough to know that death meant my father was gone. I didn't understand all of what was happening, but I did know that I'd never see him again. He was gone much too soon.

At the time of my father's death, the Church said he could not have a Catholic burial because he was divorced and had remarried. I was in the third grade and I didn't understand why there wouldn't be a funeral mass. In parochial school, whenever there was a death, the whole class would parade to church and be present for the family. My friends and classmates were not allowed to attend my father's funeral because it was not held in church. It was never talked about at school. My father had died and the Church's response was predictable. Even my family, especially my Mom, knew it could be no other way. I was confused and in a lot of pain, but I kept it locked within myself. I couldn't reveal how wrong and shameful it all felt to me. My words were frozen in my throat, and my chest ached.

My father was buried on a cold winter day. It was December 15th, the day my sister, Claire, turned sixteen. It was hard for her, hard for all of us, even my mother. I remember asking her, "Mom, why are you crying?" She said, "Linda, if it had not been for him, I would not have you." I will never forget those words and the spontaneous flashback that came with them. My mother's words softened the pain of the conversation I had overheard when I was seven. Despite her many hardships with him, she saw our loss and moved beyond the pain of the past. We were her life, her love line, and my father had given her that. My mother's acceptance, and the way she stayed with us through the whole ordeal, are etched in my brain. She had forgiven him for all the bad times. She rose above what had happened, and kept her eye on what was good. Mom did it with the Church, and she did it with my father. That part of her always amazed me.

The sun was bright, but it was still cold the morning we buried him. I remember standing at the cemetery with white mittens and hat, not believing he was gone, but believing love can hurt when a loved one leaves. Those were my thoughts as I stood at his grave. In the middle of all of this, my 10-year old heart believed that God still loved us, and I wasn't going to let the response of the church, my school, or the whole community, diminish that. As far as I was concerned, my father was in heaven. He loved life, he lived his pain in his own way, and in the end, he was kind to us. It was too late for a lot of things, but it hadn't been too late for his heart to touch ours. We all got a glimpse of what was good in him, and it stayed with us. If only he could have stayed longer.

Much of my understanding of faith and religion, and how they differ, was shaped by this event. I came to understand that God's presence is not limited by what we are taught by others. It is only limited by what we think of ourselves and our God. The Church and public opinion said my parents were divorced and therefore, bad. I instinctively knew that God was bigger than whatever circumstances happened in life. God knew my mother and father were good people.

At a young age I learned not to judge an experience or an event simply by what I had seen, because so often it was not reality. God often brings us to places of pain to reveal to us his mercy and forgiveness, and to remind us that no one can stand in judgement over others except Him. I witnessed the institutional Church stand in judgment over issues in the lives of others, and I learned that those judgements were not always absolute, and certainly, not always compassionate and merciful. I would not allow anything, not even the Church, divert me from what I saw and felt in my heart. Years later, when I joined a religious community, I realized that rules were often written to be guidelines. The mind has to learn the rules, but also interpret reality through observation, listening, and one's loving heart.

My father's death automatically rectified my mother's relationship with the Church. She was a widow, no longer a divorced woman; therefore, allowed to attend Mass. Her second marriage, performed by a justice of the peace, was never recognized by the Church; however, it was only when my stepfather died in 1979, did the Church welcome her back into the fold. She was now able to receive the sacraments, and take part in all religious activities. I remember how much that meant to her. She was so happy, and we were happy for her. In spite of everything that had happened, my mother never turned away from her faith. Her living example of faith had a profound impact on me and all of my siblings. Because of her, my own faith was built on something inside of me, and not necessarily on what the Church dictated was right or wrong. The Church once told her she was living in mortal sin because she was divorced; therefore, she should be excommunicated. Now, because she was widowed twice, they took her back. My mother's faith was truly her own because, whether the Church condemned or accepted her, she remained steadfast and never let go of her faith.

The South Berwick apartment we lived in after our brief stay in Somersworth accommodated us for a few years, then my mother decided to move closer to my maternal grandmother in a section of town called "The Landing." The Landing was comprised of a number of two-story duplex apartment houses built very close to one another. Compared to the farm, our neighbors were now an arm's reach from us. My grandmother lived in a small house behind us until she fell and broke her hip, and my mother took her in. I loved my "memere." She was the gentlest, kindest person I had ever known. She loved to crochet and knit, and I watched her make beautiful doilies and mittens for her family, friends, and anyone in need.

My grandmother was very religious and at times it seemed her faith could move mountains. Whatever was to happen in life, she'd always put in God's hands. I would often walk by her room and see her saying her prayers or reciting the rosary. The expression on her face was reverent and beautiful, and I know her simple, unwavering faith helped to fashion my own. My mother and grandmother had a very close relationship in that they were friends and really loved each other. As I got older, I had a similar relationship with my mother.

Overall, people who lived at The Landing were friendly. Our backyard was a parking lot, but we always managed to find a spot to gather and play. Our home was everyone's home; my mother had a way of allowing that to happen. The pot was never too empty for our friends or hers to stop by and have a meal with us. There was always enough. The "multiplication" I used to call it. She would say, "We don't have much, but what we have we'll share," and we did. My friends loved the ease and comfort of our home and often said, "You're so lucky."

After graduation from St. Michael's, I attended St. Joseph's Academy, an all-girl high school run by the Sisters of St. Joseph. I was involved in cheerleading, dance, Glee Club, and other activities. I enjoyed my friends, my studies, and my teachers. By then, my older sisters were married, and I baby sat for my nieces and nephews most weekends throughout high school to earn extra money. When summer came. I always had a job because, as a family, we had all learned that we must help financially. If I were not at school or work, I was generally at home helping my mother. Even without a father, our family life had become somewhat normalized, and I'd turned into a homebody. We walked wherever we needed to go, but to go beyond the town, we needed to depend on others because we didn't have a car. That was not always easy to deal with. It was difficult not being able to travel out of the immediate area on your own, or to go out with your friends. Some days it was terrible. My mother never complained about not having a car, so I thought, why should I? It was still hard, though.

As I moved into my teens, my self-esteem suddenly evaporated. Shyness covered my insecurity like some huge weeping willow tree. Getting out from underneath it seemed impossible. My shadow was dark and worthless. What I thought or felt didn't matter. Everything became strange and disconnected. The role of family clown was still mine, but beneath the laughter my life felt dry, and parched. I loved my friends, but I felt that if they really knew me, they wouldn't love me. I knew my mother loved me, but I couldn't accept that love. Accepting love was too dangerous because then I could lose it. By this time, I was too afraid of losing anything or anyone else.

The protectiveness I felt toward my mother when I was young changed to feeling responsible for her happiness. If she wanted me home to help paint, run errands, or take care of my grandmother, I would do it. It didn't matter if I had plans or wanted to do something else, I couldn't say no. When I did venture out to do something else, my mother had a subtle way of letting me know she didn't like it. Her subtle way was the silent treatment, and I hated it. My head would throb with guilt because I felt responsible that I had done something wrong. I was forever asking her if she was all right. On the other hand, there were good times, too. We were close, and when I was about fifteen, she started opening up to me and talking to me about subjects we had never visited together. I felt we were best friends. This made me feel good because I really loved her, but it also scared me because it made me feel more responsible.

My mother was not perfect, but I looked at her as if she were, and discounted the bad and the unpleasant. It took years for me to realize that I had made her into something more than what she really was.

During my sophomore year in high school, tragedy touched my family once again. My sister, Claire, and my brother-in-law, Bud, had a little girl named Sandy. During her first year, Sandy was colicky most of the time and rarely slept through the night. When she was about two years old, Claire gave birth to a little boy. She and Bud were ecstatic and named their son Thomas. Like Sandy, Tommy was also a colicky baby and my sister just figured her children weren't "sleepers." One night Claire had gotten up to give Tommy his 2 a.m. feeding and stayed with him until he fell asleep. At 6 a.m. the next morning, she looked in on him. The color was drained out of his face, and he wasn't breathing. She screamed. Bud came running from the bathroom, took one look and ran for the phone. We all gathered at their house after we received the call. My little five-week old nephew was still in his crib, a scene I'll never forget. We were all in shock. Tommy was healthy one minute and the next minute he was dead. Claire and Bud were in absolute anguish.

Tommy was in the house for a long time before the doctor and the coroner arrived to pronounce him dead, a victim of crib death. Shortly after, the funeral director came to take my nephew away. He picked Tommy up to put him into a little box and, as he did, one of his booties fell off. That one incident focused all of our grief and pain. His death was riveting. Everything seemed to go out of us at that moment, like an unrelenting tide: our breath, our minds, our hearts, and then, the pain and sorrow flooded in. It's impossible to describe the pain Claire, Bud, and the whole family experienced with the loss of Tommy.

The three-day wake before the funeral was an eternity of despair. Most people were gentle and kind, while a few made insensitive and unthinking comments to Claire and Bud. I remember one person saying, "Well, Tommy was just five weeks old, so it mustn't be as hard as when you lose an older child. You know, you haven't had as much time with him." My sister and brother-in-law were left speechless. They loved that little boy no matter what his age, and it took a very long time to get over losing him. A part of me never got over it.

I couldn't understand why this was happening, why God permitted so much pain and suffering to occur. Death was devastating and confusing. It scared me and haunted me. I felt confused and I didn't know how to answer the many questions I had. The weeping willow tree, my shyness, got bigger that year. Even if there had been someone to talk to, I didn't have the words. I only had a heart that hid everything inside and nothing came out.

I retreated more into myself and asked: is God not merciful? Does God care? Is God deaf? Does God know who I am? The image of God as a `Loving Father' was one I could no longer relate to. If God was anything like my own father, then He would also leave me. God as a `Loving Mother' was one I felt more at home with. I wanted God to be a "Her" and not a "Him." My mother believed in God's mercy and because of her, I believed I should trust God, too; however, these questions came at a very tender time of looking at life and death, and wondering. I wanted to believe God cared, but I experienced God as a void. I wrestled with my feelings, unsure of their names, and even less sure of their meaning. I struggled to say the right words, or enough words, and wondered if anyone heard. I felt empty, insecure, lonely, and without a clear vision or a strong purpose. I felt abandoned and alone with a sadness that just wouldn't go away.

Something of life always called me back. By now, I had become pretty adept at hiding my feelings and playing the clown. Detached, I automatically returned to the bubbly, lighthearted person I thought others at home and school expected of me. Tommy's death was tucked away along with everything else I couldn't talk about. My sophomore year was hell, but I made it through by laughing and making others laugh. When they laughed, I forgot how I felt.

From time to time, in my junior and senior years, I went dancing on Saturday nights with a group of friends. "Teen Haven" was South Berwick's hot spot for teenagers. It was a great place to dance and have a good time. Now and then I dated a few guys, but I wasn't really interested in any kind of intimate relationship. I wanted more out of my life and I didn't want to get trapped in South Berwick. I was saving money to possibly attend nursing school after graduation, but I wasn't exactly sure what I wanted to do. I was sure I didn't want to lose any opportunities by settling down too soon. I had seen too much, and I wanted more than that.

I graduated in June of `67, and at the end of that month my grandmother died. It was painful because I loved her very much, and she had been a real presence in our home. It was especially painful for my mother because she also lost her best friend. We were nearly all grown, and now there was no longer anyone at home for my mother to care for. She went back to work at the shoe factory where she had previously worked many years before.

Although we still didn't have a car, I was able to get out more and even got a job out of town. I commuted with friends and worked as a secretary at the Portsmouth Naval Shipyard. The question of what to do with my life left me increasingly ambivalent. I knew I wanted to work with people and, for a while, considered nursing school. As the year progressed, something else moved quietly within me. At first it was like a nudge, a whisper, that eventually became louder and louder. The question was whether or not I had a religious vocation. I went back and forth, back and forth, struggling over whether God was really calling me. At the same time, I didn't want to face growing up because it meant leaving home.

The nudge toward a religious vocation became more and more pronounced, and I quite naturally considered the Sisters of St. Joseph. They lived what I wanted, to minister — serve, and be with people. I knew I didn't have to be a nun in order to help people, but the nudge turned into a longing that begged to be filled. Something was missing in my life. It was like a big void in my chest, and I didn't know if religious life would fill it. Above all, I wanted and needed to be sure. I was so afraid of making a commitment to a life that I didn't feel sure of whether or not I could or would fit in. I shared my concerns with my sister Judy who said, "Well, Linda, what you need to do is go and talk with someone and perhaps spend some time with them." Of course I knew I needed to do that, but for a while longer, I ignored my vocational calling. A part of me just wanted to go to work, continue to be the funny one, and not pay any attention to what was going on inside of me. Well, that didn't last too long.

One day, I had had enough of my indecisiveness. I called one of the sisters I loved dearly and asked if I could see her. I went to her and shared where I was at in my life. Similar to Judy's advice, she thought it would be really important if I spent some time at the novitiate in Winslow, Maine, to see if that's what I wanted. The original novitiate was established in South Berwick in 1913, and then relocated to Auburn a year after I was born. As the community grew, the Congregation needed a bigger place and built one in Winslow in 1965. That October, as I entered my 20th year, I went to Winslow for a weekend, and found myself far away from home, not knowing anyone, and wondering what I was doing there. I met the novices, the novice director, the Provincial, and several other sisters. They were very warm and gracious and walked me through the three-story building that overlooked several acres of land. On the ground floor there was a recreation room, boiler room, laundry, cafeteria, and kitchen. The second floor housed the novice classrooms, chapel, prayer room, library, another recreation room and Provincial offices. Individual bedrooms and baths were located on the third floor. I learned that someone was hired to care for the grounds, but the sisters all participated in maintaining the building.

On the surface my visit went well, but underneath my anxiety was ever present. My biggest fears were: not knowing if God really wanted me there, and not knowing if I would fit in with the sisters. I was in the habit (no pun intended) of undertaking something new and expecting myself to know how to do it well. Even at a young age, I hadn't been able to ask for help and I placed the responsibility to do it perfectly on my own shoulders. The question was, "Could I really do this?" I came back thinking, I don't think this is where I want to be, yet, the more I reflected on my weekend there, the more I felt I really needed to give it a try. The extent of my ambivalence, however, was unnerving. I didn't want to take that step to say to my friends that this is what I wanted to do. Yet, the stirrings within me were driving me crazy. I needed to know if that was indeed where I belonged, so I thought, if this is not for me, and I don't belong, then I'll move on with my life.

I wrote to the novitiate and asked to be admitted. I had paperwork to fill out and tests to take: physical, dental, and psychological. Several weeks passed before I received my acceptance, letting me know I could enter on February 2, 1969. As I prepared to leave home, I hoped we would have the worst snowstorm of the century. It would be a sign from God saying, "Forget it, Linda." Not a chance, February 2nd turned out to be a beautiful, radiant, and glorious day. I thought, maybe this was another sign. Though family and friends were very supportive, some gave me, at most, three weeks.

My oldest sister Carol, her husband, David, and my mother drove me up to Winslow, a few miles south of Waterville and about 130 miles from home. It took us about two and a half hours to get there, but it was the longest ride I had ever taken. It was a long ride because I was so nervous. I had said goodbye to all of my friends, my sisters and brothers, nieces, and nephews. I really cherished my family and leaving them was emotionally very difficult. I had never been away from them before, and I was going to a place where I wasn't sure if I'd make it. Something in me had to let go. I had to trust that my mother would be fine, that she would be okay in my absence. I had spent most of my life protecting her, and it was painfully difficult to leave her now. At the same time, I carried a lot of excitement: the thrill of a new adventure, new experiences with people, and a way out of South Berwick. My ache and my excitement were evenly matched, and they rode side by side within me every single mile to Winslow.

The day I entered, I didn't even have a Bible or a rosary. It never occurred to me that those things might be "tools of the trade," so to speak. I just wanted to serve people, be there for them, and I only came to understand, after the fact, that God was a significant part of religious life. That wasn't my focus. I lived and functioned almost entirely from my heart, and I simply wanted to be with a group of people who wanted to have the same goal, the same thrust in life as I did. I chose the Sisters of St. Joseph because of how they were living, and what I wanted had a sameness, a resonance. It was safe. I was clear about that, but that's about all I knew.

In those days, when one entered the convent, the leaving of family and friends was a formalized condition. Family visits were allowed only at certain times and I seldom went home. I had left my past, hidden it away as with much of my life, and simply started as a new person called Sister Linda.

PART TWO
RELIGIOUS LIFE

The stories we tell can become an expression of what we feel,
a window into our own heart, a gift that reveals a part of ourselves.
The life we breathe into the story is our life;
the story we tell is our own.
For only in the course of time and relationships
have I come to an understanding of myself,
and the issue of losses as part of owning
my own unique journey.

FOUR

THE TUMULTUOUS YEARS

The late `60s and early `70s were very chaotic in religious life as they were in the rest of the country. Results of the 1962-1965 Vatican II Council were unfolding and a lot of changes were taking place in the Church. All religious communities were trying to grasp the changes, but it was like trying to hold water in your hands. It was nothing short of a major upheaval. Pope John XXIII had given Roman Catholic religious communities their marching orders. They needed to change, and to expand their thinking and their ministry to more accurately reflect the changing times and needs in society. This was a very difficult stretch for all communities, for some more than others. They were being asked to leap beyond what they had been accustomed to over the past 75 to 100 years, several centuries in some cases. This was more than a change in thinking. Individually and collectively, it was a fundamental change in identity. There was no blueprint, no road map, no footprints to follow.

For the Congregation of the Sisters of St. Joseph (CSJ), the leap spanned more than 300 years of evolving apostolic work. When the community came into existence in the 1640s, the sisters worked primarily in the southern and central regions of France. Unlike the isolated, contemplative lifestyle of their sister communities, CSJ was immersed from the onset in the trenches of humanity. They would venture into unknown neighborhoods or different districts of a city to learn the needs of the poor. They would then "set up shop" and begin ministering to them through nursing, teaching, and orphanages. Following the French Revolution in the late 1700s, the Congregation established its Mother House in Lyon, France. From there the community spread rapidly throughout Europe, and later into Mexico, India, and the United States in the early 1900s. The Sisters of St. Joseph were always inspired to be of service to people in need no matter what year or century it was. That's why they appealed to me so much. Their lifestyle, their involvement, and their spirit were what I wanted for myself. With the same courage and enthusiasm for which they had been known, CSJ moved forward with the mandate from Vatican II. The times were exciting, and at the same time, frightening on many levels.

In February of '69 the community was going through one transition after another. It was similar to a grand old mansion undergoing a complete renovation. The Administration had nothing to go by except the mandates of Vatican II, which were general, but required serious change. There was a lot of guess work involved, and most of the renovations to the CSJ were highly debated within the community. Some things worked for a time, others not at all, and the Provincial frequently modified their views. Cherished traditions, and the old ways of doing things, walked uneasily beside innovative, untested approaches to community life. During my first few weeks I encountered both.

When I first entered, a small prayer service was held for me as an acceptance into postulancy which was to last nine months. There were five young sisters ahead of me: three canonical or first year novices, and two second year novices. Canonical year is a period of contemplation and religious study while a second year novice is more actively involved in community. The end of novitiate training was observed by taking first vows. Final vows generally occurred five to nine years later; I took nine.

The novices still wore the habit, but with renewal it was decided that I would wear my regular clothes. I never thought much about what I wore until one day three of us were downtown and decided to go into a store. A woman saw us coming and opened the door for the novices who wore the habit. We all smiled at her graciously, but as I walked up behind the other novices, the woman released the door in my face. Another time there were four of us standing at an intersection, and we started to cross. Traffic stopped to allow the novices in habits to get to the other side, but started up while I was still in the street. I had to run for it! The habit did something to people that had nothing to do with respecting the individual; this was a very sensitive point for me.

A few years later, in August of '71, I received the habit when I took first vows. Shortly after, I went home for a visit. My family was generally very relaxed with each other and conversation and humor flowed easily, but when I walked in with my grey habit and veil, a sudden inhibition descended upon everyone. They quietly sat there, looking at the floor or at one another, crossing and uncrossing their legs as they shifted in their seats. It made me so uncomfortable that at one point I whipped off my veil and said, "Here I am! I haven't changed!" We had a good laugh, but the power of the cloth, rather than the person, left its impression on me. It should have been the other way around.

When I entered, religious life was changing so rapidly, the novice director wasn't exactly sure how to work the changes into my training. A few weeks into my postulancy, she extended to me a very unusual invitation. "Linda," she said, "would you like to work at our Mount St. Joseph nursing home as an aide?" The home was located about ten miles away in Waterville. I was both thrilled and stunned. It was an opportunity to work with people, and it also meant I was the first sister to ever go out in ministry during their postulancy. I couldn't wait to start.

I worked at the nursing home for six months and took courses on prayer and religious life with the novice director on my days off. It was a crazy schedule: I worked seven days, had two days off, then worked nine days and had four days off. Although I enjoyed my involvement at the nursing home, I found it difficult being the only postulant in novitiate. By nature, I preferred being a part of a group with whom I could learn. I really wanted to do well, but on my own, it was hard to tell how I was doing.

A couple of months into my job at the nursing home, I enrolled in a nurses' aide program at Seton Hospital in Waterville. My time was split between the nursing home, novitiate, and the hospital. I was eager to begin working and living my dream of nursing; however, within a few weeks I received a big lesson about who I thought I was and what I thought I could do. Desire does not guarantee success, and I learned very quickly that I wasn't cut out to be a nurse. I loved the patients and I loved working with them, but I had a very difficult time seeing people die. Death frightened me; I couldn't handle it. There was a 15-year old girl, Becky, who came to the hospital with a lump on her throat. She and I developed a rapport very quickly. They operated on her, but it was too late, and they simply closed her back up. It was cancer. It spread like wildfire, and Becky lived just a matter of months. I remember leaving her, going out, and leaning against the wall outside her room. I was choking with so many feelings that I thought I was going to faint. Emotionally, I couldn't deal with the fact that she was dying. I had a vague notion that my reaction might be due to my past, but I had little awareness. I felt faint, my skin was clammy, and I kept thinking, Oh, God! I can't do this; I can't do this. I also experienced guilt and shame for wanting to only help people who were going to live. My past and my inability to discuss my emotions, teamed to create an unwillingness to ask for help. The culture of the times seemed to render me helpless with feelings more distraught than ever over death.

One lesson after another presented itself, some minor, some more significant. One morning I was told to go in and bathe a man. I went in. He was in bed, and I simply asked, "Could you please slide your feet over and wash yourself. I'll be back shortly to wash your back." He said, "I don't have legs." We got through the bath okay, but I've never forgotten the experience. First of all, I was angry the nurses hadn't alerted me to the fact that he didn't have any legs. I thought their neglect was because I was just a student nurse's aide. The incident taught me how easily I assume. I started to learn not to assume anything. This same lesson was to come up again and again many years later when I did my chaplaincy training. For the moment, my inexperience received a rude awakening, but I learned to gradually stretch my abilities. Pretty soon my six months were over, and so were my thoughts of becoming a nurse.

In August of 1969, another unusual event happened in my religious training. The novices ahead of me were placed in various ministries, and the novice director didn't want me to remain in Winslow by myself. I was sent to St. Joseph's Day Care Center in Auburn where I worked as a teacher's aide with four-year olds, and lived in a convent with eighteen other sisters. This placement gave me an opportunity to experience the convent lifestyle first hand, and I loved it. I loved being with the sisters, eating, working, praying with them, and seeing what they were trying to live. There was a wonderful vitality among the sisters that nourished our common goal of being available and ministering to other people. I was happy, but the happiness I lived at that time was marred by two significant events that were emotionally difficult for me to handle.

There was one young sister with whom I got along with very well, but she was troubled far more than I realized. I walked into her room one day and found her lying on her bed. On her bed, an empty bottle of aspirin lay on its side. "Sister," I said pointing to the bottle, "did you take these?" She mumbled something but was incoherent. I said, "I'll be right back." I went downstairs and notified another sister in the house. She was a nurse. We pumped coffee into her and walked her until she vomited over and over. She eventually left the Congregation. Shortly after the "aspirin incident," two sisters whom I knew and cared for decided to leave the community. News of their departure was a sudden shock to my heart. I felt hurt, scared, and confused. I did the only thing I could do. I set these events aside in my mind, and I pressed on with my experience in Auburn which was positive and very supportive. Something in me seemed to thrive in a group situation, especially when tension was at a minimum. It allowed me to forget the hurt I felt about the past.

Gradually, I began to experience God as a tangible and powerful reality in my own life and the life of the sisters. The setting resonated with early memories of my mother when she instilled in us how important it was to believe and trust in God. Without that, she'd say, "Life is empty." Whatever we did, we had done as a family, and I felt God's presence in the midst of that. The association was significant because it was exactly how I felt living in Auburn. This community of like-minded, dedicated women served as a key that opened my relationship to God within religious life. It was during this time that God became the reason why I was living there. In the day care setting, I also discovered how much I loved working with children and their parents. Education, I felt, was where I belonged.

After six months in Auburn, I was transferred back to Winslow. Time was passing and my superiors felt I needed to complete my novice training. Traditionally, a novice had to physically be in the novitiate for her canonical year; however, the community was in transition, and being a novice it affected me most directly. The challenge of preparing me for religious life became even more of a dilemma because of renewal. Religious training had long been designed for a group, not for someone who was learning on their own. Five days a week, I, the lone novice, took classes in Scripture, Initiation to Religious Life, Moral Theology, Vows, Christian Life and Apostolic Life. I joined a handful of sisters for Mass, spiritual practices and assigned chores. The focus in novitiate was inner spiritual development, and I was not accustomed to the numerous periods of prayer and quiet time. This was an area about which I had very little awareness and even less experience. It was very difficult to sit still; I was a "doer." I was used to an active life involved with and ministering to other people. By nature, I was an extrovert. I had a good rapport with the novices ahead of me, but they were on mission and came back to Winslow infrequently. I often lamented to them, "I wish I wasn't alone...just to have someone to talk to..." They were surprised and said, "Oh, Linda, you're so lucky to have one-on-one training with the novice director. I would have given anything to be in your place." I smiled and thought I didn't feel lucky at all, and I would have gladly traded places with anyone. Not having a peer group focused the intensity and loneliness of training squarely on me.

Part of my frustration was due to the fact that I couldn't grasp the reasoning behind certain practices. This was no reflection on any one person, but rather on the way things were traditionally done. Everything was "in common," which meant that whatever was received from home or from someone on the outside had to be shown to the novice director. As an adult, it seemed very strange to do this. If it was known that someone else needed stationery and you received some, it went to the other person. I lived it and I did my best, but inside this common ownership seemed very strange to me. I understood the purpose was to instill detachment, and foster a diminishing, appetite for material things. In my own mind, however, I thought the real purpose of poverty was to set us free, not to make us miserable. Even though I was confused, I was committed, and there was never a thought of leaving.

On the surface, I remained cheerful and bubbly. I wanted to do everything right and follow all the rules. I really tried to live my religious life as perfectly as I could, but inside I was fighting and rebelling. I couldn't control the happy image I projected, nor could I control what I was living on the inside. I was on an emotional roller coaster, and I wasn't aware I could be anything else but my clowning self. My early days of isolation in Winslow were focused on survival. Hiding the tension between my happy exterior and troubled feelings seemed the only way I could get through it. Back then, I had no idea how debilitating those feelings had become.

Overall, this was a time of great emotional pain within the community. Renewal opened many doors and windows, along with many hearts that ached from the stretch of something new. There were many dynamic women of various ages who were willing to take risks, who forged ahead with new changes even though they were not sure of their outcome. Perhaps the vow that was most tested was obedience. Dialogue replaced obedience. Sisters were able to have input as to where they wanted to go and how they wanted to serve. It was a revolutionary concept, and even more revolutionary was that those in charge allowed it to happen. It took courage to trust the Spirit working in others to provide guidance and direction, but things couldn't change overnight. It was too big a task.

The internal structure of religious life in the past was built, more than anything else, on the foundation of obedience. One was sure one was doing God's will if one obeyed the superior. It was presumed that her judgment and voice were conduits for God's will. In obeying the superior's directives willingly, we were not only fulfilling God's will but cultivating the prized virtue of humility. The value was not in the allegiance to the person of the superior, but in the obedience to the spirit of God which was working through her. Years ago, sisters and indeed most people, never questioned authority. They accepted what was given and followed orders. The idea of thinking for oneself was not really an option because it was something that was rarely, if ever, done. A sister would never question. She was obedient, and therefore this fulfilled God's will for her.

Vatican II was a major force in moving religious communities toward a redefinition of obedience that inevitably unleashed a profound restructuring of religious life. Tremendous changes were also happening in society, and people were seriously questioning what they had previously taken as a given. The times were tumultuous for everyone.

In the early '70s my mind couldn't comprehend what all these changes meant, but my emotions picked up on the painful tension and upheaval that was whipping through the congregation. Renewal brought out unanticipated consequences in many communities. We no longer had to put our feelings and thoughts aside in the name of obedience. During this time, many sisters left their communities — "mass exodus," we called it. Some of the sisters who left my Congregation had taught me in high school, and they had had a significant impact on my vocation. Others I had met when I entered and had become quite fond of them. It was a hard time for all of us who watched them go. I shared my feelings with one sister and she said to me, "Linda, you have to remember that you didn't enter religious life for any one person. You entered for a reason. You need to keep your focus, and not let your feelings discourage your own call." Her words really helped me walk through many difficult moments when people whom I loved were leaving. Relationships were pivotal in my journey, in my life, in my walk with God. Close friends were leaving, and it tore my heart out. It was not unlike a death, this leaving and knowing that their new lives would change our relationships forever.

These disruptions shook me to the core, but I believed that God had a hand in all of it. I knew where I needed to be; I felt like I belonged and I didn't want to leave. My journey continued, I tried to understand what was happening, and to live my religious life as best I could. Months passed, and I was eager to make first vows; it meant my novitiate would be over. I then could go back into ministry and, in my view, begin to live again. I didn't know that as far as religious life was concerned, I was barely at the starting gate.

∞

FIVE
FINAL VOWS

My first vows were celebrated in a beautiful, reverent service that was held at the chapel in Winslow. I donned the habit of the Community which symbolized the spirit of poverty and simplicity I wanted to live. The year was 1971. I was 23 years old, enthusiastic, and eager to commence with the ministry my heart was set on, education. My assignment was what I had hoped for, and I returned to Auburn to teach kindergarten. I also lived with several sisters in the same building where I taught. Part of me felt like a young race horse who, after winter months spent indoors, is allowed to run in a vast open field. It was exhilarating and freeing.

For the next three years, I learned how to be a teacher by the trial and error method. I loved the children, and loved what I did, but I had a lot to learn about myself and teaching. The children, who were some of my best teachers, didn't hesitate to fill in the gaps in my inexperience. I remember the first day I went into the classroom; I wanted the children to love me, and I wanted their parents to like me. My compulsion for perfection was at an all-time high. I had my lesson plan all mapped out, had everything prepared right down to a "T;" however, by 9:00 a.m. I had gone through my entire lesson plan and then panic set it. It was a day-long program, and I thought, now what am I going to do? It was a day I shall never forget. The children walked all over me. They did it the next day, the next week, and the next month. Something was definitely wrong. If I was going to survive, I had to learn how to develop structure, discipline and some semblance of obedience. A part of me was too soft, too easy, and the children picked up on this like a blip on radar. Simply being a nice sister wasn't going to do it. Their little emotional bodies were the perfect honing devices for sensing vulnerability, but, over time, that drew out the real teacher in me.

∞

Gradually, I learned to work with and handle the children's short attention spans, the hyperactivity in some, and the rambunctiousness in others. I drew out those who seemed too quiet. The children were definitely teachable, and I was definitely able to teach once I grabbed hold of the reins and gently pulled them in. My skills grew so that I eventually became adept with slow learners and with children who had a difficult time in other classrooms. There was a compelling force in my teaching that eventually permeated everything I did with the children. It was imperative to me that every child be treated with respect, and consistently and enthusiastically encouraged in his or her ability to learn. Each child was unique and special, and as a teacher, I had the opportunity and privilege to convey that specialness to each of them throughout the school day. After several months, the children no longer walked all over me, and they developed a love for learning. They loved coming to school, and I loved being there with them. Parents, some of whom were disinterested at first, became as enthusiastic as their children about the school program. Education, I felt, was my niche.

Community life in the small Auburn convent was even more challenging than the classroom. Unlike my experience prior to novitiate, a smaller group can't always absorb tensions between two people as a larger one can. The reflex to tension I had developed when I was young, now became an obsession. Laughter was an all-consuming goal because it lifted me and others out of tough, uncomfortable feelings. I was "allergic" to both inner and outer tension, whether I was directly involved or just a bystander. Laughter, to me, was the best "antidote" to all unpleasantness. Even in my 20s, it wasn't anything I actually thought about, it was just something I did. I was gullible, playful, laughed a lot and caused others to laugh. Sometimes it was appropriate, sometimes not. The problem was, I couldn't tell the difference.

My routine for creating laughter always focused on the same target, me. I would do or use anything to make someone laugh, including my teeth. I have a narrow mouth. When my wisdom teeth emerged, they gradually pushed my teeth forward, so much so, that my upper front teeth overlapped one another. I had too many teeth for the space available, and the overbite became quite pronounced. The wisdom molars were removed when I was twenty-four, but the haphazard lineup of my other teeth remained the same. Twenty-six years later, braces corrected a lifetime of insecurity, but for a quarter of a century my "ivories" suffered the brunt of much derogatory humor by others, but mostly, the source of the ridicule came from myself.

When I smiled, which was quite often, I was all teeth. Drinking from a glass or a cup became a musical event as my teeth bounced against the top of the container. Even utensils carried their own rhythm as my teeth connected with them while negotiating food to my mouth. Self-consciousness over my toothy enamels blended with my inclination to turn anything uncomfortable into a joke or laughing matter. Often, especially at meal times, I'd poke fun at myself and inadvertently encourage others to do the same. I gave no indication that my feelings were hurt when others made fun of my teeth. Instead, I laughed with them, adding comments of my own which further embellished the inappropriate humor. My compulsion was that if I could make others laugh and change their mood, even at my own expense, I had to do it. I had done this over and over again throughout my life, and now, as much as I tried, I could not rid myself of this compulsion.

One sister in particular, was extremely sensitive and hyper alert to what people said, did, or did not do. She was plagued with self-doubt and often compared herself with others whom she perceived to be more accomplished or successful. Conflict with others often arose because her moods were unpredictable. She was happy one minute, sad and sullen the next. She did not get along with another sister, and the tension in their relationship darkened the atmosphere in the house. I automatically took on the role of buffer between the two.

The challenge with the depressed sister had another dimension which made me chronically stressed when we were together. She liked being with me and often sought out my company when she was feeling down or insecure. My antics were an anti-depressant; I made her laugh. At the same time, her self-doubt perpetuated an unconcealed jealousy of me, and alarming self-pity. "Sister Linda," she'd say, "you're such a good teacher. Why can't I be as good a teacher as you are?" While my stomach turned in knots, I would make light of her comment and say, "Oh, that's not true! Of course you're a good teacher. I've seen you in the classroom, and I know you are." I think she thought that what I was doing with the kids was really easy, and that I was the lucky one. She wasn't aware or didn't notice how much preparation and work I put into all of my classes. It wasn't luck; it was organization and work, and lots of it.

One evening she was observing me in the kitchen while I prepared dinner for the group. We were talking about different things when she said, "You're a much better cook than I am — you're so creative with your meals." I answered, "Now, Sister, you're just as good a cook as anyone in the house." Another time I was in my bedroom putting the finishing touches on a prayer service I had planned for the house. I loved creating and organizing these prayer rituals. I was good at it, and it allowed me to express the spiritual side of my nature which brought me a quiet inner joy, a rare experience. My door was open, and she stopped by to see what I was up to. She had this pouting expression on her face and said, "You're a much better community person than I am. I wish I could be more like you." In an exasperated attempt to distance myself from her and her self pity, I replied, "Look here, Sister, you're fine just the way you are. The last thing you want to do is be more like me. Believe me, you don't!" It went in one ear, and out the other. As much as I tried to help her, I never could tell her what she wanted to hear.

Inwardly, I was tormented with ambivalence and the ever-pressing need to be perfect in the community and in the classroom. Beneath my veneer of doing things well, I was slipping and sliding all over the place, and I was constantly unsure if I was doing or saying the right thing. This particular sister had a way of looking up to me for inspiration, and for new ideas to help her out. I'd think to myself, my God, never mind inspiration and new ideas. I'm still trying to figure out what to do in my own life.

I couldn't entirely blame her, because I had repeatedly come to her rescue with comic relief and inadvertently created a dependent relationship that drained me more and more as time went on. I could make her laugh, but I couldn't make her change. I couldn't be responsible for her, and I didn't have the heart to tell her, nor did I know how. If I told her, I was sure she would hate me, and that would have been unbearable. I kept telling myself, "I'm too sensitive."

I managed to accept this relationship for over a year, but then my body rebelled and I developed a major ulcer. My famous line, "All is fine," wasn't working anymore. As much as I tried, I could no longer hide the fact I wasn't fine. I was in constant pain. I couldn't keep food down. I lost weight and looked troubled. I finally sought and received medical attention. Cream of Wheat and scrambled eggs were my diet for much of that year. In addition to being a physically painful time, it was even more difficult because I had to think about Linda instead of others. That was tough. It meant I had to begin changing a lifelong habit of saying "yes" to anyone and everyone. Saying "no" was like trying to swim up Niagara Falls; nothing in me wanted to go that way. I couldn't say no, so my body mutinied by forcing me to attend to my own physical pain. This happened whenever I had overextended, or given away, too much of myself. I know I would not have begun this part of my journey if I had not been forced by my own body. The troubled sister and my ulcer were only the final incidents that screamed at me to take care of myself. I turned out to be a slow learner, and continued teaching. I was invited to move to another house. The sisters did not want me to move, but my heart and soul knew I needed a change.

I continued teaching for another year and then in the fall of '75 I attended the University of Maine at Farmington and lived with four other sisters in Jay, Maine. By taking evening and summer courses, I'd already accumulated nearly a year's worth of credit hours toward an Associate Degree in Early Childhood Education. I wanted to squeeze the rest of my requirements into one year which turned out to be an all out marathon. I was taking 19 credit hours plus a practicum. I loved learning, did well in my classes and had a good rapport with instructors and students. Within my community I was actively involved as a member of the Social Justice committee that met monthly to look at and study different political and social issues. We wrote to Congressmen, Senators, and other officials. We created a community newsletter to keep sisters informed about regional and national issues we were working on.

Overall, it was a good year in community and the sisters and I got along well. We played a lot and laughed even more. I loved to fool around and found myself doing things to perk up the atmosphere, whether it needed it or not. I teased and joked in order to get a rise out of people. Once when another sister and I were cleaning up after the evening meal, and I was at my command post as dish washer, I thought of having a little fun. I took my hand out of the dishwater and flicked my fingers at the sister who was drying the dishes. She'd react, and I'd laugh. I'd go back to washing and then I'd do it again. After the third or fourth time, she said, "Okay, Linda, you've had it!" She grabbed a glassful of water and before I could get away, she poured it right over my head. And then we both doubled over laughing.

At another time, a different sister, this one taller and stronger than I, did not consider my antics funny. Instead of playing along, she became increasingly irritated with every flick of dishwater. The more she got irritated, the more I continued. After the fifth or sixth time, she threw her towel on the counter and said, "That's it, Linda. That's it!" I had turned around, worried she'd leave, but she had something else in mind. She suddenly picked me up and sat me down in the dishwater. I'll never forget it. I was screaming and laughing so hard, tears were streaming down my face. It caused a commotion in the house, and I overheard a sister in the other room give a status report to another: "Oh, Linda is at it again, but she really got it this time. So-and-so plopped her in the sink!" One way or another, they'd end up laughing. I had reverted to my previous habit of "entertaining" that allowed me to stay clear of any real introspection.

I'd like to say I engaged in my dishwater routine just a few times, but I rarely fooled around just a little. Everything I did, related to humor, tipped the scale to excess. At the time, I didn't know of any other way to be. I know I frustrated some and irritated others, but I never heard anyone say they didn't want to live with me because of that. In my mind, that meant I fit, I belonged, and that's what kept me going.

In May of `76, I left Farmington with my Associate Degree in Early Childhood Education. I returned to the day care center in Auburn with lots of ideas and new strategies for working with the children. Two teacher's aides and I worked as a team which I loved. We worked hard. We had fun, and the children thrived in the atmosphere we created. At the end of the academic year in Auburn, I returned to college and became a fulltime undergraduate student at the University of Maine in Gorham. Final vows were coming up, and I wanted to finish my education so I could focus all my attention on preparing for the "big event." There was also a part of me that feared the decision-making process and the inevitable questions that rose to challenge me: Was this life-long commitment to community for me? Was I good enough? Did I really fit in? Was I doing the right thing? Did God really want me?

While at school in Gorham, I lived in an apartment with two other sisters who worked in nearby parishes. We were all very involved and working hard at what we were doing. Our first year together was good; but things changed during the second year. There were unsettling changes everywhere.

At home, my 20-year old cousin, Donna, was diagnosed with an aggressive brain tumor. The sudden onset of the cancer left her immediate family in terrible shock, which made it difficult for them to grasp the fact that she was dying. I made numerous trips home during that time. In my house, those sisters with whom I lived and loved moved on to other houses and ministries, and other sisters moved in. A sister, whom I dearly loved and respected as a close friend, left the community for a year's leave of absence. The loss was very difficult to take. I knew a leave of absence offered her a window of relief much like an escape valve on a pressure cooker. A leave of absence was the community's way of supporting and working with a sister who didn't want to leave altogether, but desperately needed a "time out." Wrestling with one's calling, God, or intense unresolved family issues emerged more among the younger sisters than the older sisters who entered years before Vatican II was ever thought of. Though I felt my friend would eventually return, which she did, her departure and absence tore at my heart. No matter how often it happened, I never got used to people leaving.

Residential disruptions combined with actual and pending loss made for an emotionally difficult year. I felt lifeless and without energy. Aside from immersing myself in schoolwork and periodic trips home, I tired easily and napped whenever I could. I thought my classes were the source of my fatigue. It never occurred to me that something else might be causing it.

It wasn't laughter that kept me afloat that year, but prayer, personal and communal. Whomever I lived with, we met in the evening to recite the "Office," the Prayer of the Church. Our weekly community meetings included a prayer service that was orchestrated by a different person each week. Over the years I'd also developed a relationship with personal prayer where for an hour a day I felt grounded and anchored. While changes and transitions swirled around me, prayer drew me to my center, that silent still point in the middle of a storm. For me, prayer was the key to everything. It allowed me to step aside from the effects of my personal and community life. It was a way of recharging my heart and my determination to live religious life as perfectly as I could. In prayer I found respite, solace, but not necessarily peace.

My focus in life was to live the gospels, the words of Jesus, which carried so many layers of meaning and understanding. I'd read a line from Scripture, and then let that line speak to me. I also gravitated to the Psalms where David echoed my own distress calls to God. "My God, my God, why have you deserted me?" he wrote, "How far from saving me, the words I groan! I call all day, my God, but you never answer, all night long, I call and cannot rest." (Psalm 22:1-2) I wanted so much to be happy, to connect with God and with others, but I had a deep gnawing feeling that something inside of me was missing. My prayers were often in the form of supplications. I'd say, "God, please help me to know what to do; how to be faithful; how to be the best sister I can." I felt God was so present to everyone else, but not to me. It took me a very long time to realize that I wasn't even present to myself. Sometimes in painful exasperation, I'd look up and say, "You know, God, this isn't a `Sound of Music' experience!" At those times, I hoped God had a sense of humor.

I lived that second year by taking one day at a time. One night, I prayed Psalm 63:1-2, "O God, you are my God whom I seek; for you my flesh pines and my soul thirsts like the earth, parched, lifeless and without water." I was feeling so alone that the words penetrated my heart right to the core. In desperation, I went to the prayer room and told God, "I need to feel your love. Something has got to happen. Please help me." I remained still hoping for something, anything, to happen. Suddenly, as I finished, the center of my emotions began to fill up and overfill me. All those months of mechanical prayer fell like water down a fall. My whole being became filled with an intense love from God; I felt heat radiating through every pore. In those brief moments, I knew with certainty that God loved me and was present in my vulnerable, questioning self. It was enough to keep me going for a long time.

I managed to complete my classes and, in June of '79, graduated with honors with a B.S. in Early Childhood Education. I took a position for a year as a teacher at a Head Start Program located in the rural town of Jay. My involvement included going into the home and working with the parents whose children were in our program. I was also in the classroom with pre-school children, and I thrived. I loved the experience of combining my work with children and their parents. My health, and especially my focus, were restored to a deeper, more grounded place within myself. I was grateful because it was time to take a good look at my approaching final vows.

It took me longer than most, nine years, to make my final vows. The delay was due in part to my own ambivalence, the time needed to complete my education, and to the radical changes in the community. From my first day as a postulant, the community was in transition and still was eleven years later. I knew I could teach, I knew I wanted to stay, but I was in transition too, and I was searching for clarity within myself. On some level, the fragility of my self esteem matched the community's crisis with its own identity. Obedience and the overall direction of the community were core issues for both me and the membership at large. Some of us wanted change, others were more hesitant, but the process of renewal was hard for all.

With the end of Vatican II in 1966, the approach toward obedience had been completely restructured to include individual and collective consensus. Blind, unquestioning obedience was gone. In addition to open dialogue regarding placement, the community fostered the development of individual gifts among its members. Emphasis on individual growth, started in the '70s, was in full momentum by the time I prepared for my final vows in 1980. Once individual gifts were developed, the challenge for the community was how to use those gifts collectively to shape a unique and creative working presence in the world. Here was the painful spur in this ingenious plan. Supporting the development of individual gifts gave rise to a strong sense of individualism and independence. The very qualities that nourished individual gifts inadvertently created problems for the fledgling blueprint of the community's larger picture. The question remained: how do individual gifts fit into a common goal? The difficulty lay in making the transition from independence to inter-dependence and inter-relatedness for the good of the whole. The Provincial Team and others struggled courageously for a harmony and unity of purpose that we all wanted but couldn't seem to make happen.

My personal work at that time was focused on final vows and surviving by doing the right thing. I wanted to be certain this was where God was calling me. It was the same ambivalent thread that had tied me in knots when I was debating whether or not to enter. I took everything so seriously and debated endlessly with myself before saying "yes." This desire for certainty replayed itself 15 years later when I struggled so hard with the decision to leave the community. I strove for integrity in my commitment, but every decision became more painful than those before.

As I prepared for final vows in August of 1980, I explored all the ins and outs of my understanding and of my relationship to living out my commitment. I lived the vows of obedience, celibacy, and poverty as meaningfully and as consciously as possible. To me, they were not an end in themselves. Rather, the vows carried a vibrancy which I reverenced in myself and in others. I was committed to the Spirit in each vow as opposed to the words written on a piece of paper.

I understood the vow of obedience as a sensitive and attentive listening to God, to others, and myself. There was a threesome here. I'd bring my issue before God in prayer and ask, "What do you want me to do?" If my inner experience was agitated, such as, "I want to do this! I want to do this! This is what I want!" I knew then that this was "of Linda" and not of God. But if I sensed a peace and an acceptance, that was my cue of God's discernment in the matter. I'd bring that discernment to authority, talk about it, listen to what the leadership would have to say, and then decide. Sometimes my decision was to do something I really didn't want, and by deciding to override my preference, I ministered as a Sister of St. Joseph to the greater whole. Other times, my overall discernment led me to a different path from authority's preference. It was all about making a choice with the Spirit of God at its center.

Of all the vows, celibacy was most difficult. I wanted to feel and be awake to everything I was giving and giving up. It was not a question of giving up my womanhood, my sexuality, but of making a conscious and willing choice of how I would live the expression of my love for others. As I matured in community, celibacy actually became more challenging and difficult. A sister once commented, "It gets easier as you get older." I replied, "Honey, for me, it gets harder, not easier." I wanted to feel the loss, the absence of physical love, because I wanted to really experience what I was giving up. At the same time, I could love totally and unconditionally the people I was working with and ministering to. The two seemed to go hand in hand, and that's how I lived it.

The vow of poverty also held a unique twist for me. For me, the vow of poverty exceeded a material distinction and was not about being "poor." Poverty was accepting the beauty of all of God's gifts and appreciating them within a simple lifestyle. My community provided me with insurance, food, a roof over my head, a job, and a lifestyle I loved. My vow of poverty was a striving to live each day in a spirit of gratitude and serving my neighbor with acceptance, judging actions and not people themselves. It was being available and freely giving of my time, my resources and my talents. Poverty was not a material issue for me and never was.

Of the three vows, obedience was my biggest challenge. I was caught in my compulsion to be a perfect nun who followed through on everything as perfectly as I could, yet, underneath lay a dormant renegade who slowly awakened with each passing year in community. A lot of people didn't know this part of me because I had concealed it so well, even from myself. I had some vague notion that being told what to do made me vulnerable to getting hurt. I wanted people to think I could make it. I felt like I fit in, I didn't want to leave, and the slightest thought of ever being asked to leave terrified me. I pursued the role of being "good," the perfect nun who was determined to assure her continued membership.

Final vows marked the completion of a nine year sojourn since my first vows as a sister of St. Joseph. God's grace and benevolence were never far from me or those around me. I meandered unknowingly, yet trustingly, through the various ministries offered in the community. Through those experiences, a maturation of my own faith took root. Living through pain, loss of friends, and creative involvement helped me to develop a measure of womanhood in religious life. It wasn't easy. None of it was easy. Through it all, the community supported my growing pains into adulthood and my fledgling spirituality into a more grounded reality of God's authentic presence within myself and within others. I shall never forget what they did for me, never.

SIX
WINSLOW

At the time of my final vows, I was approaching a crossroads in my ministry. I loved teaching, I was good at it, but in the last few years I had been increasingly drawn to work with children in my classroom who had been abused. To pursue this avenue required returning to school and getting a master's degree in social work. I was also experiencing a pull in the direction of deepening my spirituality. How, and in what way, I did not know. I was not even sure whether a Master's in Social Work and working with abused children was where I wanted to be or where God was calling me. It made sense to get some hands-on experience before enrolling full time into a master's program. There were no residential settings for children available in Maine, but there were in the Boston area.

I also had a personal reason for wanting to go to Boston. Two of our sisters, who were close friends, were living and going to school in Boston. They were considered a little avant-garde, rebels who were always trying something new and different. They gave the administration a headache from time to time, but to me they offered a certain kind of daring and excitement I was unaccustomed to. They were living among the poor in a housing project, and I wanted to be there "in community" with them. I had a desire to move beyond the boundaries of Maine and to experience life in, what was to me, a larger, totally unexplored world. I approached the community with my desire to work there for several months with abused children. With the community's blessing, I moved to Boston in August of 1980 and got a job as a house mother in a halfway home for boys. Here, I came face to face with "reality" in a way I was not prepared for.

There were 25 boys in all, ranging in age from 10 to 15 years old. They were hardcore children who had already lived through a great deal of abuse and trauma in their short lives. The stories I heard broke my heart. One of the boys had been seriously abused by his stepfather. The man had battered the boy's head with a baseball bat. Several of the boys were coming from homes where both parents were imprisoned, and they ended up on the streets before coming to the halfway house. In every case, they were very angry, bitter, hurt, and mistrustful of adults.

∞

For many reasons, the boys had a hard time with women. As a soft-spoken, inexperienced, new, female, staff member, I was a quick target for their projection of unresolved issues with the mother figure in their lives. It happened almost immediately. On my first day, I received my first black eye. I was playing football with the boys outside and one of the boys "accidentally" hit me in the eye. I showed up for work the next day with an unbelievable shiner.

Day time was always filled with unpredictable tension and the threat of violent behavior. We never knew what would set the boys off. Nighttime was different. I found it was the best time for me to have a one-on-one experience with them, as many of their defenses were lowered. Most of the boys couldn't handle physical contact during the day; even a pat on the back wasn't tolerated. At bedtime, however, their defenses were down. They allowed me to talk gently and encouragingly as I tucked them in, and I sensed they actually looked forward to it. They sought the nurturing and warmth much as two-year olds would, but when morning came, there were more bouts with anger and hatred. It didn't take me long to realize that love was not enough to heal these boys. They required structure, discipline, and therapy that were beyond my ability. It wasn't too bad with the younger ones, but the older boys were very much beyond my capabilities.

I worked closely with one little boy named Michael, and I thought we were developing a stable relationship. One night something set Michael off and his anger spun him out of control. He was jumping up and down on his bed, cursing and running through the halls, and causing a lot of chaos among the other boys. I was alone on the floor and was on my way to him when Michael spotted me and ducked into a large cupboard. The cupboard had an iron door with a handle on the inside rather than outside (I never understood why). Michael had the door ajar enough for me to get my fingers in. As I reached in, he purposely closed the door on my fingers. Excruciating pain shot through me. I tried to stay calm and kept repeating to him, "Michael, open the door....open the door, Michael." He wouldn't. My eyes began to water as the pressure from the door caused my fingers to turn a dark blue. I finally said more firmly and loudly, "Michael, OPEN THE DOOR!!" and he did. I pulled my hand out, and called for another staff person. My fingers were bruised but not broken. "Love is not enough," echoed through my mind later that night. I was clearly not where I belonged.

I was approaching three months on the job when it became quite evident to me that I needed to get another job that hopefully involved younger children with whom I felt I could work. I learned of another children's center in Boston that had a daytime, early childhood position which it was seeking to fill. This was an educational-therapeutic day care program that worked primarily with three, four, and five-year old children who otherwise would be on the street. The position sounded ideal. There were about 100 applicants for the position, so I was thrilled when the program manager called to let me know I was hired and to plan on starting in three weeks. I immediately gave notice at the halfway home and whispered a prayer of gratitude to God for pointing me in the right direction. I soon learned that the right direction does not always coincide with what we would choose for ourselves.

A week into my three-week notice, the children's center called to let me know that funding for my position had fallen through and hiring was being put on hold until February. Panic set in. I would be out of a job in two weeks. It was December and I needed another job to carry me over until February. I scrambled for work and found a temporary position, starting in January, at a local bank. In mid-December, I made a weekend trip to Winslow with one of the sisters with whom I was living. In 1972, the novitiate had been moved to Lewiston and the building in Winslow, aside from the Provincial offices, was converted into a Christian Life Center. As we drove up the driveway to the Provincialate, a heavy feeling came over me. I turned to the other sister and said, "Goodness, I don't think I will ever be able to come back here to live. It's just not where I'd want to be."

A few weeks later, I would regret those words. At Christmas time, one of the sisters returning home from a skiing trip had been killed in a car accident. She had been administrator of the Christian Life Center and her death was a real loss to the community, both spiritually and professionally.

After the funeral, the Provincial requested to see me. She asked if I would come to Winslow and serve as assistant administrator at the Center. My first thought was, Oh, God, not this! This was not something I wanted, but a conversation I'd had with a sister before making final vows flashed into my mind. She had asked, "If the community ever needs you to render a service, would you accept?" I had replied, "Yes, of course I would." So here I was faced with my own words. The seconds seemed like hours as the Provincial awaited my answer. I didn't have a job to speak of, and I knew I could render this service. I agreed to come back to Maine.

I returned to Boston to pack my things and while there received a phone call from the children's center letting me know funds had been restored and I could begin work immediately. My heart was sinking as I replied, "I'm sorry, but..." I hung up the phone and thought how pivotal the moment was in making a choice. I felt conflict and anger between the needs of the community and my own needs which were, as yet, not really clear to me. I loved the community, I wanted to help, but I was ambivalent about returning to central Maine. I was just beginning to expand my wings, and once in Winslow, I felt I'd have to tuck them in again. In hindsight, my life would have unfolded very differently if I had stayed in Boston. Confrontation with the reality of my life, and how I was living it as a Sister of St.

Joseph, would have happened much sooner. As it was, part of me believed God had a hand in the unusual timing of these events and the experiences which were to follow.

My move to Winslow in January of `81 coincided with yet another onset of painful changes. The sudden loss of the former administrator shocked the community to its core. Especially at the Provincialate, the sisters were grief stricken for months. The Provincial Team had no sooner repositioned people when, one by one, strategic people left the community. The vocation director was the first to leave, followed a few months later by the formation director. A number of other sisters left during and after this same time. We all suffered through these departures. Emotionally, they were very much like recurring death experiences. No one could really stop these traumatic upheavals. The Provincial Team worked hard to maintain the community's vision and fragile stability during the painful transitions, and they were somewhat successful.

Although I did not always agree, I had a lot of respect for this Provincial Team. In the years following Vatican II, their administrative and spiritual responsibilities on behalf of the community were extremely difficult, and at times, seemingly impossible. Three sisters elected for a six-year term made up the team. The position of Provincial was full time while the other two were half time. The team was responsible for the fidelity of the province to its mission. They maintained close working ties with the Mother House in France and with our mission in Brazil. They met and worked with individual and groups of sisters, helped to resolve problems, and explored new apostolic interests. They negotiated residential changes and requests for continuing education and training for spiritual development. This team also worked with older sisters who wanted to slow down the changes brought on by renewal, as well as with younger sisters who thought the changes were not fast enough nor deep enough. For them, maintaining a balance between the two was a fulltime endeavor.

In Winslow I worked with a sister who, in addition to being administrator of the Center, was also part of the Provincial Team. The pressures of her dual responsibilities were great, and I wanted to assist and support her in anyway that I could. She was an exceptionally bright, articulate woman, gifted with perception and clarity, especially in group situations. Her capacity for vision and for understanding the dynamics of religious life in the throes of renewal were nothing short of sublime. I had seen her in action at numerous meetings where, in the midst of a heated debate, she would come out with an astute observation or a clarification of the issue that gave miraculous resolution to the conflict. I loved her dearly and had a profound respect and admiration for the quality of her mind and ability to focus. I wasn't aware, however, how stressful it could be for her to relate personally to others.

The Christian Life Center was an exceptionally busy place. Groups were coming and going all the time: community facilitated retreats, marriage encounter weekends, engagement workshops, cancer support and other self-help groups. Several churches and religious groups also rented space for their activities. As assistant administrator, my responsibilities were essentially to prepare meeting rooms and sleeping accommodations for groups coming in, and cleaning up after they left. It was primarily a behind the scenes support position that I could do well but, much as I tried, my heart wasn't in it. I repeatedly had to talk myself into folding sheets and towels and doing the repetitive tasks. I assured myself that I was doing something worthwhile, but over time it became increasingly difficult to "will" myself into the job. I carried on effectively, but felt lifeless and without purpose.

The administrator and I kept the Center running smoothly. Our skills were complementary when it came to managing groups, and we worked well as a team. I naturally move toward people and like to engage and develop personal relationships through conversation. I loved putting people at ease, making them feel welcomed and at home. She, on the other hand, managed the business end, solved problems when they arose, and kept the Center on course.

I admired the administrator's mind and her capacity for clarity and focus. She'd get right to the point, and said what needed to be said. She never minced words. I think she appreciated my ability to get along with people, because this was not her strong point. There were seven other sisters who lived at the Center, and from time to time, the administrator experienced some interpersonal difficulties with them. I understood both sides. She could be blunt and to the point, which would sometimes offend others. I'd say, "Not everyone understands how you're thinking it through. It would help if you explained things a little more." Or, when asked, I'd say, "Don't be too hard. Be gentle. You need to be softer." I looked up to her and wanted people to like her. I covered up for her and tried to smooth things over. I was always concerned about her and wanted to relieve some of her pressure. Something in me always seemed to hone in on people who needed help. At least I thought they needed help, so it made me feel important to take care of them. Little by little, I started to see glimpses of this lifelong obsession, and quite honestly, I preferred not to see it.

The administrator also had a reclusive, withdrawn streak in her. She'd lapse into silence, much the same as my mother would when she was angry or disappointed with me. This was very unnerving. I'd be frantic to get even a trickle of communication going. Something in me would noticeably motivate me to try harder, I would be more cheerful, more helpful. At times, even with others, I think I was a nuisance.

One day, another sister with whom I worked confronted my behavior. She said, "Linda, you're so unreal. You always talk `pretty.' Everything is wonderful to you when it isn't. Get real." My mouth kind of dropped, and my mind went blank. Her words stung, but I couldn't understand what she was saying. I walked away thinking I don't talk pretty, I'm just talking the way I always have. Everyone in my family talked like this. What was so wrong about seeing the brighter side of life? Isn't it better to be happy than sad? Isn't it better to give people hope? I couldn't fathom what she was saying, and the more I thought about it, the worse I felt. I didn't know how to be any other way. I was doing the best I could, but I started ruminating. Maybe my way wasn't good enough; maybe I don't really fit in; maybe. I told myself, go fold some towels, Linda, and I did. Think about something else, Linda, and I did.

I continued my private little crusade on behalf of the administrator for quite a while until I became vaguely aware that I couldn't do or give anymore. I thought my lifelessness was due to my job, and the solution was to do something else. I hated to leave her; a part of me felt as if I were being disloyal and abandoning my responsibilities. In the back of my mind I thought I hadn't tried hard enough, but it was also clear to me, I needed a change. The truth, of which I was not aware, was how much of myself I had abandoned in order to help others. It would take another ten years for that truth to reveal itself.

I remained at the Center for two years, and then in September of `84, I went to Auburn to teach four-year olds. In 1985, I became program director at day care. I worked with parents and staff in developing and evaluating curriculum, and designed a language program for the three to five year olds. The program taught the children the basics and readiness skills for reading. I enjoyed the challenge of the program, the interaction with adults, and I especially loved working with the children once more.

During the summer of 1985, four other sisters and I traveled to the community's Mother House in Lyon, France to attend a month-long international session designed for younger professed sisters. The General Team leadership in France wanted us to experience the sacred grounds and holy origins of the community. We walked the same halls as our Foundress, Mother St. John, and prayed in her room. Through French translators we learned firsthand how she courageously rebuilt the community after the French Revolution. The focus was on renewal and recommitment of our individual and collective callings. I loved the diversity and flavor of so many sisters from different countries. We were united under one goal, one spirit of ministry and dedication. It was a group experience I shall never forget.

Meetings, workshops, and pilgrimages to other cloisters and cathedrals, which I loved, were interspersed with periods of quiet and solitude, which challenged me further. Returning to the source, walking the community's sacred roots and making it my own, moved me in a powerful way. Throughout the month, and thereafter, echoes of the welcoming address reverberated in my thoughts. "Remember," the General Superior said, "no religious vocation is given once and for all. It unfolds gradually and is deepened at every stage of life." These words revitalized and reconfirmed the essential truth of my relationship with God, and how that relationship was being expressed in my life and in this particular religious Congregation.

The part of this pilgrimage that had the most profound influence on me was our time spent at Lourdes, a town in southwest France. Between February 11th and July 16th, 1858, the Virgin Mary appeared on eighteen separate occasions to a 14-year old, illiterate, peasant girl named Bernadette Soubirous. Since that time, pilgrims from all over the world have prayed before the famous grotto with its healing spring waters. Outside the grotto, thousands upon thousands of pilgrims meander through or around hundreds of souvenir and commercial vendors who repeatedly call one over to buy this or that memento. Once inside the grotto, the silence and the reverence are so powerful that one is immediately drawn into prayer.

I sat in front of the grotto for hours watching an uninterrupted procession of pilgrims of every nationality, parents wheeling their crippled children, and older children carting their maimed or deformed parents before the statue of Mary. That day, I saw hundreds of people in emotional and physical pain walk in only to leave with a quiet expression of peace and joy for having touched the holy ground of

Lourdes. That day, I learned that a healing of the spirit was as miraculous as a healing of the body. There are many ceremonies throughout each day of the year at Lourdes, but the most moving is the candlelit procession of the rosary held every night at 8:30. The Hail Mary is prayed aloud in many different languages, but the reverence and individual candle flames of thousands merge into a beautiful oneness that transcends all differences in religion and culture. That night I experienced and united with Mary in a most profound way. In my heart I told her, I know you will be with me. Whatever I have to go through, I know you will be there. Little did I know of the additional losses that were waiting for me on the horizon, and that I would need her very much in my life.

I returned to Auburn in time for the school year. My spirit and soul were re-energized and spirituality took on a more grounded dimension. God became more of a vital, living presence in my consciousness. On another level, I felt that time was running out for me in education. I had given a number of years to teaching, but now there was a yearning to move more deeply into spirituality, though I was not sure of the direction it would take me.

Earlier that summer I'd attended a workshop given by Matthew Fox, a Dominican priest, who shared his vision and commitment to what he called "creation spirituality." Fox described his Institute in Culture and Creation Spirituality (ICCS), which he founded in 1976 at Holy Names College in Oakland, California. ICCS offered a 9-month, intensive, Master's program in Creation Spirituality. There was an earthiness to the values and ideals of creation spirituality that attracted me. My summer in France only increased my desire to attend. From what I knew, I believed Fox's program would strengthen and solidify the spirituality I felt growing in my heart. I remained as program director while also exploring with the community the possibility of enrolling at ICCS. Suddenly, all plans came to a halt — my body was falling apart.

I had been having terrible problems with my menstrual cycle, and was hospitalized on several occasions to have a D&C, a laparoscopy, and recurring cysts removed. I was told, I did not ovulate because benign cysts kept forming on my ovaries. They were removed and then grew back, double their original size. I was losing weight and menstruating 30 out of 31 days. I was prone to colds and infections because my immune system was so stressed, and I came down with what I thought was strep throat.

The doctor informed me, "You don't have strep throat, Linda, you have tonsillitis. I know you've had your tonsils removed, but the infection is located right where your tonsils were." The doctor paused for a moment, looked directly at me. I could tell he was trying to tell me something I didn't want to hear. He said, "Look, Linda, you need to make a decision. Either you have a hysterectomy and go on hormone replacement therapy, or you continue having surgery to have the cysts removed. It's your choice, but I would recommend the hysterectomy."

Repeated surgeries were no longer an option, because every time I went in, I became weaker when I came out. I knew he was right, but I felt a dull, aching fear whenever the word hysterectomy was mentioned. I went for a second opinion and the doctor confirmed the original diagnosis. Surgery was finally scheduled for April of '86. I was 38 years old, the same age my mother was when she had her hysterectomy. Prior to surgery, I was in emotional chaos. Fear floated on top of my pending loss like oil on water. My mind understood the medical necessity for the operation, but my heart and my body rebelled with a heated rage of having to be mutilated in order to heal. My reaction confused some of the women whom I sought out for support. Several echoed a similar refrain, such as, "Oh, I wish I were going through that so I wouldn't have my period every month." Another woman who'd had a hysterectomy casually said, "Nothing to worry about...it's a piece of cake." I wanted to scream, but I didn't. Instead, I walked away overwhelmed with frustration for not being able to communicate how I really felt.

I was terrified of the loss. I hated the fact that the part of my body that carried the potential for life was going to be carved out of me permanently. Even though I had been a sister for 18 years, I cherished my body's potential ability to create life. I feared the loss of control over my body and how it would react after surgery. Would I get fat; grow old young; and have hot flashes? All the reading in the world, and intelligent conversation, did not eliminate my anxiety and fear. I was losing something I couldn't see, but emotionally I was very much in touch with what it meant. I have since learned that my fears and terrors were not unlike many other women in similar situations. In those days there was little real conversation about such "personal matters."

Fortunately, the hysterectomy was partial; the uterus was removed, and the ovaries were left intact. This meant menopause would not be an abrupt experience, and I would not need longterm estrogen replacement therapy. I remember touching the scar and being aware of an emptiness and a feeling of powerlessness. A sense that something holy had been removed from my body collided with the reality of mutilation. Integrating these senses emotionally, psychologically, and spiritually took time — longer than I would have imagined.

I am aware that not all women face the same fears when confronted with this kind of surgery. I am also aware that all the preparation in the world does not eliminate the need for going through the stages of loss, many of which are triggered by the surgery itself. The intensity of my reaction would have happened regardless of whether I was in community, married, or single. My reaction was my reaction. Even though the operation brought relief to a serious medical situation, hysterectomy meant a loss to a part of myself. My usual response was to bypass the emotional pain, but this time I couldn't. I wasn't sure how to go on to a new life with a different body.

For me, talking through my conflicting fears was life saving; facing the issue of loss, very important; being affirmed as a woman, critical. A few women philosophized the hysterectomy and said, "Now you can give birth to other kinds of things." Unfortunately, that did not resonate for me. My close friends, however, allowed me to be worried about being a woman first, a religious second. I was never advised to go and pray to overcome my pain. Rather, they encouraged me to see and find Christ within the experience. Several women, both in and out of the community who had had hysterectomies, were exceptionally sensitive in their response to me. They understood the anguish I felt and allowed me to express it as best as I could. With them, I fully experienced the depth and empathy of women ministering to women. Through these friends, the feminine aspect of God's Presence became clearly visible to me. It was beautiful and healing.

As spring turned to summer, my body gradually restored itself. During my recuperation, I continued to explore the possibility of enrolling in Matthew Fox's creation spirituality program. Something in my soul prompted the desire to be there and really immerse myself in the opportunity. The community, however, held a different position which I understood. Matthew Fox was a rather controversial figure, and more conservative groups preferred to keep a distance from his programs. As it turned out, plans for heading West would be abruptly postponed. My surgical experience in the spring was only a forerunner for the losses that were to shatter my family that summer and fall.

PART THREE
HEART DISRUPTIONS

The experience of death is
an experience of separation, a tearing apart.
The patterns of one's life and heart are sundered.
Mending involves sorrow, the acknowledgment of brokenness,
and hope somewhere in the future for
a wholeness once again.

SEVEN
LOSSES

My recuperation was marked by the untimely death of my brother Bobby. It was July 14th, 1986. He was at a father-son baseball game with his 13-year old son, Timmy. Bobby was in the bleachers, choosing to sit the game out because he was not at all well. In the previous four years he had suffered two heart attacks which left his heart damaged and fragile. The team was minus one dad, so they asked Bobby if he would pinch hit. He should not have stepped up to the plate. I have often thought, had I been there, I would have chained him to the bleachers

Bobby felt the need to do this for himself and for Timmy. That's the kind of person he was. He got up to bat, connected with the ball, and to everyone's surprise, he hit a home run. He ran the bases, people were cheering, but when he arrived at home plate, he collapsed. Amidst the shock and commotion of the crowd, Timmy ran to his dad and tried to wake him.

Bobby never regained consciousness. While waiting for help, people were milling around in disbelief and hovering over him. The ambulance arrived, but Bobby died on the way to the hospital. Either before or while they moved Bobby from the playing field, someone took his wallet. The wallet was found a few days later outside the ball park. The money was gone.

When I got the phone call about Bobby, the shock mobilized me to pull myself together physically and emotionally. I wanted to be fully present for Bobby's family and for my mother and my family. There was no time to grieve. I felt people needed me to be strong and in control. I kept busy seeing to many details: the liturgy, the service, and being supportive for others. A few weeks later at a seven-day retreat in East Gloucester, Massachusetts, I finally realized Bobby was gone.

It didn't come all at once, but in waves that at the moment overwhelmed me with emotional pain. Death was so dark, so final. The sadness that ran through me ran deep. When the tears finally came, I cried for everyone and everything. I cried for Bobby, for his years with alcohol, and for past events that drove him to it. I cried for my family, my mother and her trials, my father, and the sisters I cherished who'd left community. I was flooded with a sea of memories and emotions, and in the center of it was Bobby. He was the only clear thing I could see.

I learned that memory can sometimes be a healing balm for grief. I recalled a conversation I'd had with Bobby back in February, a few months before my surgery. He was being hospitalized for a second heart attack, and I felt I needed to see him and be there for him. That day, Bobby really talked, and for the first time I saw who he was.

I walked into his hospital room and said, "Bobby, how are you?" Bobby started talking and I did not open my mouth once, which was a feat in and of itself. "Linda," he said, "I don't want to die. I'm 47 years old and I've done a lot in my life. I'm not afraid of dying, but the hardest thing about it is leaving people here. I want to see Timmy graduate from grammar school (which he did). I'd like to see him graduate from college, but I don't think that's going to happen." He paused a long time, then said, "I just look at life so differently now."

Bobby valued life, and he was now looking at where it was taking him — his death. He was aware that the people he had loved, and had since passed away, would be there waiting for him. He talked about our father, our "memere" and others. Then he said, "Linda, I'm going to miss you. I'm going to miss Dee (his wife), I'm going to miss Mom, and...and...," he named us all. This side of him was not a side I had known. He had always joked with everybody and made light of everything. I had never seen him serious about anything, and here he was talking about his life and death, what he loved and didn't love. Bobby was considered the black sheep of the family. After he left home, he was always in trouble because of one thing or another. He drank a great deal and was jailed several times because of the wrong choices he made. My mother always worried about him. It pained her deeply to see how his life was going, or not going. Now, it was as if he was completely removed from all of that turmoil.

Beginning with his first heart attack four years before, I came to know Bobby as I'd never known him. This time, he was completely open, totally clear. By nature, Bobby was a meticulous and organized man. His previous heart attack had changed his life dramatically and brought him closer to his family, his wife, and Timmy.

With this attack, he struggled with the deeper meaning of his existence. He struggled with purpose and lived the hard question: "I'm not afraid of dying," he said again, "but why do I have to die so young?" One of his great desires was to live life fully up until the final moment. "I want to live until I die," he said. "I've had a chance to look at my life, and I want to savor each moment I can," and he had.

On that seven-day retreat, I often played and re-played the scene of Bobby running the bases as I imagined it. I'm sure he must have experienced some pressure, some pain in his chest, but he continued running until he made it to home plate. The whole scene of running, coming in to home plate, and dying, seemed so significant. Bobby died the way he wanted to: awake, moving, and engaged in life. In my heart, I believed God was at home plate waiting for him. I don't think Timmy will ever forget the experience of his dad running for him, for both of them.

The generational thread of death in my family was more than a coincidence. When my father died, Bobby was with him; when Bobby died, Timmy was with him. My father and Bobby were both 48 when their hearts beat for the last time. Interestingly, I am 48 years old as I write this story. They were able to address the darker side of their lives before they died. The only difference was that Bobby knew it was coming. He had his first heart attack when he was 44, shortly after the sudden death of his 18-year-old son from a previous marriage who was killed in a motorcycle accident. Bobby's second attack came three and a half years later. His third one was fatal. Bobby showed me that dying was not separate from living. Bobby's life, his story, and the memory of him sharing his truth, touched me as a point of grace. It will always be with me.

The long summer ended, and the smell of fall was in the air. The Maine foliage, which I had always loved, was nearing the end of its colorful radiance. I remember marveling at the fragrance of the changing seasons, the dance of falling leaves. Death and loss had been such a large part of my past months. I was trying to grasp the pain and darkness, and I welcomed the fall as a reflection of what I was living.

Once again, I approached the community with my desire to go to California and attend Matthew Fox's institute. The Provincial Team was very reticent and preferred that I not involve myself in Fox's creation spirituality program. I persisted, and letter after letter was written. Finally in October, I received a favorable response, and the blessing to apply for the following year. I was ecstatic. I called my mother to tell her the good news, and she was thrilled for me.

By the start of November, I was in full swing at the day care center in Auburn. It was November 3rd. I had had a tough day at work and was in my room praying while some of the sisters were preparing dinner. At about 5:15, someone in the house came to tell me my sister Carol was on the phone. When I got on the phone Carol said, "Linda, Mom's gone." I asked, "Well, where did she go?" She said, again, "Linda, Mom's gone." By the second "she's gone," I understood, but I didn't want to believe it. I was still dealing with Bobby's death, and I couldn't believe it was true. My whole being fell into a state of shock...not my Mom! I kept thinking, Oh, God, it can't be true. It's too fast! It's too sudden! She was my mom, my dad, and my best friend, and now she was taken from me all at once! Nothing could control my grief and sorrow.

I was leaning against the wall and I just collapsed and slid all the way down. I couldn't scream loud enough. My whole body was aching. I had no control. A deep, dark void encircled my body, and I just screamed. The sisters helped me. Someone grabbed the phone while the others got on the floor with me. They just held me. I was beside myself. I kept saying, "NO! NO! NO! NO!!!," as if "no" was going to change anything. My world fell out from under me, and I was lost in pain. Every part of my body ached and felt cold. Denial swept over me, and I hoped this was just a bad dream from which I'd wake up and the pain, the void, would go away. It wasn't a dream, it was real.

Two sisters drove me to my mother's home that night. The next three days were the hardest days of my life. Everyone in my family was in a state of shock. We were coping the best way we could, taking care of arrangements and making funeral plans, but it was very, very hard. When I first arrived at my mother's place, we decided that I'd stay there for the next several days with my sister Cora who also lived out of town. On the second night Cora said to me, "Linda, I really can't stay here. It's just too hard to be here without Mom. Why don't we stay at Claire and Bud's house?" I said, "I can't. I need to stay here. If you need to go, you go. I have to stay here. This home, my home, is going to be closed, and I want to spend as much time here as I can. I need to be as near as I can to Mom." Cora listened and understood. "No," she said, "I'm not going to leave." We stayed together all three nights, and then we went to my sister Claire's home.

I learned that my mother died on November 2nd from what appeared to be congestive heart failure. Evidently, it was very quick. My sister had talked with her in the morning and everything seemed fine. Every Sunday night my aunt and her daughter would go to my mother's and play cards. It was a Sunday evening ritual. My mother would bake something during the day, cookies or some sweets, which they would have, and then spend the evening playing cards. Everyone in the family knew that my mother played cards on Sunday night. Our visits were early in the day, to avoid interrupting her cherished time.

She died sometime between 2 and 4 o'clock on Sunday afternoon. The TV was on. It looked as if she had been lying on the couch. She probably experienced some discomfort, got up quickly and fell, dying instantly. That evening my aunt called my mother to arrange for the card game, and when there was no answer, thought my mother must be out. My aunt and my cousin drove by the house, saw that there were no lights on, and thought my mother was at one of my sisters' or my younger brother's house. On Monday, November 3rd, my sister Carol stopped by after work to have a cup of coffee with my mother. She knocked on the door, found it unlocked, heard the TV, and said, "Hi, Mom," but there was no answer. She walked through the kitchen to the living room, looked over, and saw my mother on the floor. Carol immediately went over and moved the coffee table out of the way. It had toppled over when my mother fell. She tried to shake her. She said she knew my mother was dead but didn't want to believe it. She got up, walked around, came back and tried to shake my mother again. Then she knew. She called 911 and then her daughter Patty. Soon a number of people showed up. The police came and interrogated Carol because she had moved my mother. Then my other sisters Claire, Judy, Cora and my brother Charlie came. They were living our family's worse nightmare.

The wake lasted one afternoon and one night. Many people came because my mother was really well loved. It was nice to know and see that, but meeting and greeting people was hard. The funeral, which took place on November 7th, was harder still. We woke up that morning to an unusually bizarre storm for that time of the year. There was snow and freezing rain, and farther north it was snowing much like a northeaster. Sisters from my community, who lived up north, had started out, but were forced to turn back, because the storm was raging, and the roads were too treacherous. A few of the sisters had come the night before and stayed at our community in nearby Kittery. The weather also prevented us from having a ceremony at the gravesite, but the funeral was poignantly beautiful. The love, reverence, and the pain of saying goodbye to my mother, are memories that will always be with me.

Shortly after the funeral service, I drove back to my mother's gravesite to pick up some flowers. As I approached the cemetery, the snow had turned to rain and it was falling gently on the windshield. It had been well over two hours since the funeral, and I presumed my mother would already be buried. Upon entering the cemetary, I realized that I had yet to confront the grave. It would be the second time in a matter of months, and the pain of it was searing my insides. There was an older man who was just beginning to bury my mother's coffin. I couldn't believe my eyes, and knew in my heart I could not leave. I watched him throw one shovelful of dirt after another into the hole that now held my mother. I watched him cover the woman that gifted me with life. I wanted to jump in to be with her. "Oh, God," I whispered to myself, "I can't stand this pain." The pain squeezed my heart like a vise grip and wouldn't let go.

I remember bending down to take some dirt into my right hand and a white rose in the other. Gently, I threw them into the grave. I stayed until the old man had finished. I remember thinking to myself, I'm not going to make it. I have to live the reality of this nightmare now. Deep within my heart I heard the words, "Choose life, Linda; I gifted you with life, and now you need to choose it!" It was my mother's legacy and blessing to me. My knees were weak, but I managed to walk back to the car, got in, and sat there. I now stood alone as a woman. I felt the arms of many embrace me, yet the pain of aloneness and 'Linda-less-ness' enveloped me. A handful of dirt and a white rose thrown into the grave brought home the realization that she was really gone, and I had never had the chance to say goodbye.

My mother was buried on a Thursday, and by the following Monday her apartment was cleared out. We needed to do that, we needed to bring closure, but it was so fast. It was very hard on everyone. Her things needed to be distributed, but I didn't want anything except her rosary. That Monday, I returned the keys to her apartment. I walked into the empty house and stood there. There was a tiny spot on the carpet where my mother had vomited after she fell. I remember standing in the living room and looking at that spot where she lay for the last time. With tears in my eyes, I said goodbye to my mom and my home. I put the keys down, walked out, and closed the door.

In my heart, it was my home I was leaving. Whenever I had come to South Berwick, I stayed with my mother. My sisters and brother all had their own homes, but this was my home, and now I was closing this chapter of my life. I felt both orphaned and homeless. My siblings were wonderful to me. Claire and Bud extended an open invitation, and each of them gave me a key to their homes. They assured me I would always have a place to stay whenever I came to town. My sister Cora often said, "We're not much, but we're damned hard to beat." It was true, we have always been there for one another. We're all different, have had our own experiences, and have our own way of dealing and coping with things; but when adversity or disappointment was present, I could not ask for a more tender, supportive group of people. I felt truly blessed to be a part of them, and they a part of me.

As I had experienced with Bobby, recent memories of my mother flooded my heart and mind. I had been home a few weeks before she died. She always treated me like a princess when I had visited, and took great joy in preparing my favorite foods and doing all kinds of baking. That evening, we had talked as she was preparing dinner. At one point, she had stopped and looked at me and said, "Linda, do you know the one thing I pray for?" I said, "What's that, Mom?" She replied, "The one thing I pray for is that I don't die alone." My heart skipped a beat because I couldn't even begin to think of losing her; it was not something I had thought I could handle. Shaking off the feeling, I had said to her, "Mom, there are six of us, so you will never die alone. Besides, you're going to live to be a hundred. You'll never die alone, because there will always be one of us here with you." I had to live with those words now. I could never promise that to someone again, because I lived through hell remembering those words. I began to wonder if she had been trying to tell me something, but I had to let go of those thoughts, because they were just too painful. She had died alone and was undiscovered for more than twenty-four hours. I didn't know if she suffered before she died, but the doctor told us she died quickly. I held that thought in my heart, knowing she was not long in pain.

Four days before she died, she called to wish me a happy birthday. I had been happy to hear from her. Before ending our call, I had wished her a happy birthday for birthing me, and giving me life. I told her I loved her. I thanked God for the opportunity to tell her that much.

For me, 1986 was a hellish year. Surgery tore my body open. Bobby's passing tore open the sadness I'd long kept hidden from myself, and my mother's death tore apart the very fabric of what kept me together, her love. I felt shredded, and out of the tears and unyielding pain, I finally saw death as it is. Anyone and anything that lives must die. I had understood life and death as two distinct and separate experiences, but were they really? Instead, was it possible that they represented a continuum, a process of growth? The question haunted me, plagued me, took root inside of me. This was my starting point with "creation spirituality." I felt that the California experience would help to integrate what I had been living the past year. The Provincial Team, however, saw things differently.

EIGHT
VISION QUEST

The months following my mother's death were beyond anything I'd ever experienced. Other than the classroom where I functioned well, I kept a low profile, cried a great deal, and spent a lot of time in my room. It was nearly impossible for me to pray or to really talk with anyone. I felt stricken with grief and overwhelmed with sadness, and I thought it would never end. Emotionally, I was always in pain. There was nothing I, nor anyone else, could do to soften its crushing grip on my heart and chest. Even God let me be. I knew that I had lost my mother, but I'd come to the understanding that I'd also lost a part of myself as well. I honestly believed, however, that part of my healing was waiting for me out west in Matthew Fox's Creation Spirituality program.

My mother's permanent absence changed me inside. It happened naturally, and at first, almost imperceptibly. I began giving myself permission to do the things I wanted to do. It was sort of an adolescent streak that I had never lived through. When it came to Fox's institute, it never occurred to me that I wouldn't attend.

The Provincial Team wanted to protect me. The past year was filled with so many losses, they wanted me to look for a place closer to home, so I would have access and support from family and community. The team had always felt a little uneasy with Fox's unconventional program, and now more than ever, they felt other programs were better suited for me. I knew that I really had to make my position clear. I suggested to them that I was discerning enough to know where I was being called and what I desired to do for myself, namely to attend the Institute in Culture and Creation Spirituality (ICCS) Masters program. I appreciated and understood the team's concern for my bereavement process, but I told them, I can mourn in California just as well as here. I also wanted to deepen and nourish my spirituality, and I firmly believed Creation Spirituality would provide that opportunity. I asked that they bless my request. At first, they didn't.

I understood the Provincial Team's position, but it was frustrating. Their concern for me was not only for my grieving, but also for my spiritual and vocational well being. There is always a risk of loss involved in letting a sister, especially a bereaved one, be so far removed from the community. Though the team didn't agree with my point of view, they remained open and respectful of my position and what I had to say. In my heart, I felt we would eventually work things out. At the time, my request was causing somewhat of a stir in the community. I think some of the sisters thought my California plan was a little too "far out." In a year I reasoned, no one is going to give a damn. They'll greet me with open arms and have all kinds of questions about my experience. It simply is not going to matter what they think now.

The team and I went back and forth, and after much negotiating with prayerful discernment, we worked out an agreement. The team wanted me to be anchored in solid, theological precepts before going to California. They strongly recommended I take two courses on the sacraments that were being offered that summer at St. Michael's, a well known Catholic college in Winooski, Vermont. I also agreed to continue discernment, as to becoming administrator of the Christian Life Center and vocation director for the community, upon my return from California. Finally, my request was approved. I ended the school year at day care in early June, and then attended St. Michael's for the rest of June and July.

Before leaving for Oakland in August, I was bedridden for nine days. My back had often acted like a barometer for my stress level. I'd be overloaded with stress, and no one would know it, least of all me, then my back would rebel with excruciating muscle spasms. It forced me to take time off, this time, nine days. My body was stressed, but my spirit was excited and determined to get to California.

A few weeks later, barely mobile enough to travel, I flew to San Francisco and taxied to Holy Names College, home of ICCS. The cab driver, a sweet man, carried my luggage in for me. When I was finally alone in my room, I sat down at my desk and cried for a full five minutes, then I washed my face, walked out into the hall, and introduced myself to everybody.

I immediately felt at home with the program and the people in it. Creation Spirituality brings one through what is called "via negativa, positiva," a journey in which a person cycles through many different places in the heart, producing "creativa." It happened very quickly for me. I faced my mourning by telling stories through art, movement, and words. I walked through the inevitability of death and dying, gained insight into my own mortality, and came to a greater understanding of what I had been through in the past year. My perceptions changed as a result of this. I looked at life experiences not as blessings, but as experiences, good and bad, that blessed my life. I will never be able to say that my hysterectomy, my brother's death, and my mother's death were blessings, because they hurt too much. We don't go through loss, pain and emptiness and say they're blessings; however, I could say these events blessed my life, because as a result of them, I became a different person.

I learned to be with other people in pain, and to be silent and receptive, because there's nothing one can say sometimes. I learned to be there with my heart, first.

ICCS attracted many different kinds of people which both surprised and delighted me. I came to know atheists, agnostics, people afflicted with AIDS, gays and lesbians, Buddhists, Protestants, and people from other religions. There were priests who were gay, people who were struggling with religious life, Native Americans, and people involved in the healing arts and alternative medicines. The differences, rather than separating us, brought us closer together in our brokenness, pain, and personal struggles.

One particular class helped us to articulate our pain in a very powerful way. It was the beginning of the African Dance class, and like members of an African community, we stood in a circle. Each, in turn, was invited to stand in the middle of the circle and share their story. I was nervous, but I thought I could manage to tell a little bit about my life. I was startled when we were told to share our likes and dislikes about our bodies! My God, I never really liked my body. I suddenly felt as if I were on the edge of a precipice, and to open myself up before these men and women about my body was like leaping into a bottomless space. I was more than frightened. My nerves felt as if they'd jump out of my pores, and I had to remind myself to breathe. I knew I couldn't last long in this agitated state. I thought, Linda, just go ahead and do it, and then it will be over. I volunteered to go first. When I stepped into the circle, my heart pounded loudly and my hands and legs visibly trembled with nervous energy. I knew I was alive, and my body seemed to scream with the desire to share its wounds and vulnerabilities.

This was the first time I had ever described, aloud, how my skin really felt. I was scared. I began with my face, my eyes, then my nose. My voice cracked as I admitted how unhappy I was with my teeth — another first. I loved my hands. I loved to touch and to hold, and I believed hands have a way of blessing. As we spoke we had to touch each part of our body: face, neck, breasts, stomach, legs, each blessed part. Pain tore at my heart as I spoke about the part of me that had a scar. My womb had been removed. My potential for birthing was taken from me, and I had felt an incredible emptiness. As I gave voice to my pain, tears streamed down my face. I stood, hands covering below my stomach where my womb once was, feeling the full impact of brokenness and loss. Suddenly, amidst the pain and the tears came a new feeling of strength, of owning and reclaiming my womanness. Naming who I was, describing the parts of my body that I loved, parts that I had lost, parts that shamed me, brought a new focus for the first time. Through my body's story, I was beginning to see who I was and who I was becoming. One by one, the others came forward like myself. We all cried as we revealed our woundedness, but in that woundedness, the light of divinity showed through our humanity, our oneness.

With this group of people, the Scriptures really came alive for me. Compassion and acceptance for the soul integrity of each was always present, always palpable. We were all different; but in matters of the heart, we were one. We learned to support one another during seminars and practicums. Together we delved into Creation Spirituality, Spiritual Psychology, Spiritual Direction, and Deep Ecumenism. We also took classes in Dreams and Liberation, Feminist Awakening, and The Mystics, namely Meister Eckhart, Hildegard of Bingen, Julian of Norwich, and Mechtild of Magdeburg. We shared classes in Tai Chi, Dances for Universal Peace, Arts as Healing, Creative Writing, African Dance, and the Wisdom of Native American Spirituality. Each day was an experience of wonder, expansiveness, and deeper grounding in the self.

The most memorable experience of my training occurred during the Native American Spirituality class. The class was taught by a wonderful, spirit-filled person named Buck Ghost Horse. He walked us through a number of Native American traditions which included one ritual where adolescent boys were asked to make a vision quest. Each boy would spend a 24 hour period alone on a mountain, praying and seeking a meaningful quest for his life. To accomplish this, each needed to confront something in himself that, once faced, would allow him to jump from adolescence into manhood. Many of the people in my class were very interested in participating in this kind of experience.

Native American tradition is grounded in nature and life experiences. They use ordinary things, and make them meaningful. Nature speaks to the Native American from the trees, rocks, grass, sand, rainbows, eagles, leaves, and even worms. Everything has a purpose, a meaning. I was very attracted to this tradition because it spoke to me of nature, of life, of all of creation and the cosmos. These were things I had loved profoundly since I was a little girl. In this class, the essence of spirituality would be heightened for me, as well as deepened.

Buck Ghost Horse spoke more about the vision quest and announced that it would be offered to students who wanted to make one. I thought to myself, I can't do that! You'd never get me on a mountain, exposed to the elements for 24 hours, and besides, I'm scared to death of darkness! A few days later I had a dream. In the dream, Buck Ghost Horse came to me and offered the vision quest saying how important it would be for me to make it. I woke up with the importance of my vision quest dominating my thoughts. I even said aloud, "No, not me. I'm not going to make this vision quest," but the dream stayed with me. It would not go away and made me think. I wondered why I had the dream. For several days, I wrestled with the dream and its message, and then I thought, why not? Maybe this is something that would bring me to a different place in my journey.

Not everyone could make a vision quest. We needed to have a purposeful reason for wanting to do it. We couldn't just go up to Buck Ghost Horse and say we thought it would be a good idea to make a vision quest. We needed to know what was going on within ourselves.

I decided to trust the dream, and requested to make the vision quest. I had all the information I needed on how to prepare and ready one's self for the experience. The date was set, but when I checked my calendar, I realized that my family was coming from Maine to visit for a week. Part of the preparation for the vision quest was fasting and contemplating for three days, which would really interfere with my being with my family. As it turned out, many students were planning their vacations the same week my family was due to arrive, so Buck rescheduled the vision quest for April 16th. This meant that it would now fall on April 17th, Bobby's birthday. It would have been his 50th. I thought, oh my God, this is a real sign for me that this is right.

I arranged to meet with Buck, and talked with him about why I wanted to make the vision quest. I told him about the dream, about my struggle, and my resolve to make one. "The purpose," I told him, "is to touch the darkness within my own heart and confront that." Buck agreed with me. Later, there were ten of us who met as a group with Buck Ghost Horse to talk further about what we were doing and where the vision quest would take place. We were asked to find our spot in the hills just outside of Oakland, a spot where we would spend 24 hours. With help from my sponsor (we each had one), I found a spot that offered a spectacular view of Oakland. It was gorgeous. The spot I had chosen was in the open, and my sponsor said, "No, Linda, if it's a hot day you're going to be in the sun, so maybe you should back up." I moved back a bit so the woods were behind me and the overview of the city was still before me.

I fasted for two days with only liquids: juice, bouillon, coffee, and water. The body has to be purified before making a vision quest. Fasting is thought to be a way of purifying and cleansing the body of toxic energy and material. Cleansing certainly does happen. The first day I thought, this is going to be bad, because I don't fast very well. When I don't eat, I usually get a headache. From day one, I talked aloud to myself: "This is what you're going to do, Linda. You're going to be fasting. You're not going to be putting any solid food in your mouth. You're doing this for Linda, and you're doing this to come in touch with what you really need to come in touch with. You're not going to be sick; you're going to be fine." That's how I went into it, and I was fine.

On the third day, I got up early. It was Saturday morning. We met at a sweat lodge. This was a new experience for me. In the middle of a tepee, a hole was dug and filled with heated rocks. By pouring water on the rocks, steam and heat filled the tepee like a sauna, but it felt much hotter than a sauna. The heat and steam really opened and penetrated each pore, cleansing not only our pores, but seemingly every cell in our body. While this ritual cleansing was taking place, we prayed. Many Native Americans pray to a spirit bird, the hawk or the eagle. I could relate with some, but not all of their ways of getting closer to their spirit god. I took what my tradition had given me, and prayed to Jesus and the spirit of my mother.

We left the sweat lodge, and were taken to the mountain by our sponsor. I brought 150 prayer ties I had made. Each represented someone I would pray for during my vision quest. The ties were filled with tobacco and strung together on a very long string. The string was used to mark the perimeter of my 6'x3' prayer space. Our sponsor would join us in prayer during the entire 24 hour period, and there would always be someone at the base of the hill in prayer with us. People in the dorm, and others who knew we were making this vision quest, would also pray for us and with us. The reverence generated from all these prayers would be very powerful.

I first laid down a piece of plastic and then arranged the 150 prayer ties around me in my rectangular space. All of the people symbolized by the prayer ties were with me, therefore I was not alone. That was my safety. We were not allowed to leave our space, but remain in the middle of it for 24 hours. The only things I had with me were a blanket, my prayer stick, my mother's memorial card with her picture on it, and my brother Bobby's picture. I also had a tiny rock that my sponsor gave to me that was very symbolic.

Accompanied by my sponsor, my prayer ties in place, I was ready to start. I remembered Buck telling me that it would be very important to remove our shoes as we entered our holy space, our holy ground. I took my sneakers off, handed them to my sponsor, and told her to take them with her. There I was, standing on my holy ground, surrounded by my prayer ties, in my stocking feet. The day was overcast. We had arrived on the mountain about 11:30 a.m., which meant I would be there until 11:30 a.m. the next day. We said goodbye to one another, and I watched my sponsor walk away. We could stay in only two positions, standing or kneeling. I chose to stand, and then I began.

I started to pray. I prayed for everybody, for people I knew and didn't know, for the poor, the sick, for the people at the college, and for members of my family. I prayed for all the sisters, each one by name. I prayed and prayed, and then I reached a point where I could pray no longer. It was still daylight and I thought, now, what am I going to do? I tried to think only about what was occurring now, and became really observant of everything: the sky, the rocks, the ground, various insects, a little ant that was walking up a leaf. All living and nonliving things really impressed themselves on me, and I felt grateful.

It was at this point I said to myself, I want a sign. I really want a sign that will let me know my Mom and my brother are at peace. Please, God, send me a sign. I looked up and saw a bird flying around. The bird came right over to me, and I got chills all over my body. Another thought came to mind, if it's really true that both Mom and Bobby are at peace, I want two birds. Suddenly two birds appeared and flew right around me. I had to make sure, so I pushed my request a little further and thought, if this is a real sign; a real sign that Mom and Bobby are at peace, then those birds are going to fly right over my head. I couldn't believe it. The two birds circled back and flew right over my head. Tears welled up and I started to cry. I said aloud, "Oh, my God, Linda, this is my sign that Mom and Bobby are at peace and that they are right here with me." The birds then flew off towards the horizon. That was the beginning of something very holy for me in my sacred place.

The day gradually went by. I found, after a while, that extended ritual prayers didn't seem important, so I focused on what was meaningful for me. I began using the Hail Mary as a holy mantra. Hail Mary, full of grace, the Lord is with thee. Blessed art thou among women. I kept praying those words over, and over. I noticed it was getting towards dusk and the day was coming to an end, so I began to pray more earnestly: "Creator, God, I'm here and I want to go through this experience. Please do not send any two-legged or four-legged creatures my way, because I'm not the bravest person, and I will die. Please, God, please don't send anyone. I'm really trying to do the best I can." Dusk was setting in. I was standing and holding my prayer stick when I saw at a distance a four-legged creature. I took my prayer stick and pointed it at the creature. "Please go away," I said, "I am so scared, so please go away." By then, the creature, which turned out to be a coyote, was running towards me and stopped directly in front of me. He suddenly veered sideways, and then disappeared into the woods. My heart was beating wildly and a part of me wanted to run, but there was no place to go. It was getting dark, and I didn't know the mountain. I thought, okay, Linda, this happened. Jesus, Mom, and Bobby are with you and they promised no harm would come to you while you're on your vision quest. You need to know that you are secure from here to heaven, and nothing will enter your space if you stay in your space. I literally put my safety in their hands, and did not think about that coyote for the rest of the night.

Usually the weather is glorious in California, but not on this particular night. It was drizzling, the wind was picking up, and it was one of the coldest nights we had had. The wind was crossing my sacred ground and hitting me in the face. It was cold, and by this time, so was the ground. I was standing in stocking feet on my piece of plastic. My feet, then my legs, then my whole body became cold, and there was no way to get warm, even with a blanket. The drizzle and overcast completely shielded the moon and the stars. It was pitch dark. I was frightened, and then I remembered; I was here to face my darkness.

Like it or not, I was in darkness both within and without. It was cold, windy, and so dark. I had no idea of time or what part of the night it was. I was on my knees praying and felt I knew a little of what Jesus went through when he was on the mountain by himself. The fear kept mounting, and I began feeling nauseous. I started to vomit, but it was dry heaves because there was nothing in my stomach. My head was throbbing. I could feel myself sinking into my fear, and I didn't know if I could make it. I kept thinking, here I am on this mountain, I did this to myself, nobody put me here, and they're going to find me dead tomorrow morning because I'm so sick. I thought again of Jesus when he was tempted, and I understood something about that experience. There was such a great desire to give up. I had never been tempted like that before. The fear that I would not make it through the night was excruciating.

I put my head down, wrapped myself in a ball, and closed my eyes. It was so cold. My prayers seemed weak, and a kind of surrender moved through me, then I had an experience of Jesus. I felt His presence right next to me, and I was flooded with something indescribable. The presence was Jesus, but He came to me in the form of Buck Ghost Horse, a man of strength, of courage, and of gentleness. The form then turned back into Jesus, and He put his arm around me. Something in me let go, melted away. I sat up. My headache was gone. I no longer felt frightened or scared of the dark. There are no words to describe this experience except that it was profoundly spiritual and so revealing of the power of Jesus and of God in my life.

I prayed. I prayed with my heart a wordless prayer of gratitude. I continued praying and when I looked up, I saw a line in the sky. I said, "Thank you, God, the night is over. Thank you, God, the day is beginning." Everything was lifting, and then suddenly the curtain was drawn and it was pitch dark again. I had no idea of time and my mind struggled with the thought that it's probably just midnight...probably just a cloud. I don't know what time it is. I started praying again, and suddenly it was morning. I will never forget that moment. I had been through an experience that had taken me into the darkest place in my heart. I had the profound understanding that if I stayed through the night, if I stayed with the experience of pain, something would happen. It's important to stay and not run. I needed to go through the darkness in order to see the light. Daylight came and it was beautiful.

I realized that this was the gift of my vision quest. It was going through the dark, seeing where it took me, and what it brought out of me. It's a place that I had to go through using all of my strength. I learned that no matter how long the night is, no matter how dark the night is or how fearful it might be, if I went through it, the light of day would come. Day happened, and it brought me home to myself. That was my gift. That was my epiphany.

I watched the sun come up, and it was exquisite. Surprisingly, I watched myself in the snare of another temptation when I thought to myself, God, I can quit now. I've been through the night; alleluia; praise God; it's over! My goal was to continue praying until my sponsor came for me. I learned that that can be as hard to go through, to wait through, as any part of the vision quest, because a part of you justifies that you have completed the hard times, and now it is time to move on. Wrong! It was time to simply continue doing what I had been doing which was praying. I prayed as deeply as I could, and wonderful things began to happen. I communed with some members of the winged insect family. There were hornets, bumblebees, and flies who were swarming about saying hello to the morning, just as I. There was a beautiful orange butterfly that kept flying all around me and wouldn't leave me for the longest time. Its presence was almost angelic, and I felt blessings emanating from its wings right into my holy space. I was grateful, I was happy, I felt wiser and closer to who I really was in the truest sense of the word. I continued observing, watching, and feeling gratitude that I had lived through it and learned so much.

My sponsor finally came for me. We were all to meet at another sweat lodge off the mountain. As we left the area, it was suggested that we not say a word, which was a little beyond me. I could not stop talking. At the entrance of the sweat lodge, I remembered that I had had no food for three days. I entered the lodge, and it was extremely hot, the rocks were crackling and the steam rose in such thickness. It was a different experience this time. I loved it, found it refreshing, cleansing, and was not lightheaded when I emerged into the sunlight. I went back to my room and showered. We were cautioned to be careful what we ate, because our stomachs did not have anything in them. I had a hamburger and fries, and I felt wonderful; however, later, back in my room, I felt completely drained. I wrote in my journal for a little bit, went to bed early, and woke up early the next morning. I wrote again about the experience. We didn't share the experience with anyone for a week, just allowed it to sit within us and let it unfold. At the end of the week, I met with Buck Ghost Horse and talked at length about my experience.

My vision quest was truly an exceptional experience. I would never say to people that this is what they have to do in order to seek what they need to find within their heart because it is a very difficult experience, but if someone wanted to go through it, it is an experience he or she will never, ever forget.

I remembered how upset my family was with me for undertaking the vision quest. They were concerned and scared for my well-being because at the time there had been several stabbings and killings in the hills surrounding Oakland. They had said to me, "Linda, go in your room, close the door, stay there for 24 hours and pray. It will have the same effect." I knew my sisters loved me, but I had to go through this. I had said to them, "I'm doing this because I need to touch a part of myself and nature," and I did. I touched the elements, I touched my heart and soul, I touched my vulnerability, and I touched the gift of life. Above all, I touched the presence of God, and it left me different inside.

My nine months in Oakland allowed me to really live creation spirituality. I'd confronted my own darkness and fear along with death, loss, and grief. I learned that grieving takes a long time. No one can say to another it's over and done with. I am still to this day grieving. I have lived it, and it is mine. There are moments when memories surface and the sadness is there. Although it is different, I sometimes mourn my mother more today than the day she died. I miss her face; I miss her smile; I miss her touch as much now as I did then, but time is a healer. Time allows other people to walk in, to hold and be with you, and allow you to do what you need to do in your journey with loss. It's interesting how I was later drawn to work with people who are dying. Without creation spirituality, I would have never been able to be open to that experience. As I flew back home, back to Winslow, back to the Christian Life Center, I knew something powerful had changed inside of me. I did not know how it would manifest itself, but in time I was certain it would, and indeed it did.

PART FOUR
THE STRUGGLE

I have new beginnings and choices, yet I ask myself:
Who am I to myself? Where am I going? What do I choose?
A lifetime of fear prevents you from being who you really are.
It's similar to dragging a cement block behind you;
you struggle, seemingly forever,
until one day you realize you simply can't do it anymore.

NINE
INTERFAITH

It was not easy to return to Winslow after the Oakland experience. Much had changed within me. I felt I was no longer the same person. I didn't know then how these changes would express themselves because they had not fully evolved, but I knew they were there. There was little time for transition, however, and I was immediately plunged into my responsibilities as administrator of the Christian Life Center and vocation director for the community. These dual roles were a whole new experience and demanded all my attention. As administrator of the Center, I coordinated the numerous groups that were coming and going, and helped to oversee maintenance of the building and grounds. Once again, the need to be focused was important because I realized I was not an administrator type, but I was given a job to do, and I was determined to give my all to that end.

As vocation director, I met and worked with women who were interested in religious life. I shared with them the values of the community, our Constitution, and the unique charisma expressed by the Sisters of St. Joseph. The vocation director offered support until the woman expressed a desire to enter religious life. The director would then make a recommendation to the formation director. I attended workshops specifically designed for this kind of work and expanded our focus with new brochures and printed material highlighting the mission of the Sisters of St. Joseph. I educated the sisters in the community about our vocational program, and gave presentations and talks to groups of interested women. Vocation retreats and weekends at the Center created a reverent atmosphere for exploring religious life and the call one felt toward it. I enjoyed this work, but as with other congregations, the community was experiencing diminishing interest and a lack of vocations. It was a trend that saddened many of us. No matter how many workshops we took or how creative our brochures and retreats were, we couldn't seem to generate more vocations. As I busied myself with a new retreat program or a new idea for a pamphlet, I ignored the encroaching reality we all had difficulty seeing.

∞

During the first year, the Center was an extremely busy place, but a decline in the number of groups coming slowly became apparent in the second year. The popularity of marriage encounters dwindled and an increased number of parishes organized their own engaged encounters. Various support groups, including cancer support groups, were launched by other organizations. The areas which had been administered to by the Center almost exclusively, now were being addressed by others. Our numbers began to fall. We were feeling the pinch as more groups who rented space from us were unable to afford the weekend costs at the Center. We were hard-pressed by the changing times, the increasing availability of services like ours, and the fragile economy.

I functioned well as administrator and as vocation director, but a part of me felt a return of the lifelessness I'd experienced when I first worked at the Center. I yearned to be more engaged with people rather than with overseeing programs that facilitated and supported others. I had agreed and was committed to these jobs for a period of time, and I wanted to honor that, but I also needed something else. Unlike before, there were only so many towels an administrator could fold.

This led to me becoming a volunteer hospice worker in my "spare time" through a program affiliated with the local visiting nurse association. Hospice volunteers were part of an interdisciplinary team that included a doctor, nurse, social worker, and home health aide. The volunteer provided respite care for the primary care person, emotional support and companionship to the patient and family, and helped with meal preparation and simple tasks or errands. For a few hours a week, the program gave me a way to be personally involved with people.

I completed the nine-week certification course, and then worked with several patients over a year's time. The program required a minimum of four hours a week. We were assigned one patient at a time and followed that person until he or she died. Some patients lived for only one or two weeks after becoming involved with hospice. I became very close to one woman who lived for several months. I'd prepare light lunches or whatever she thought her stomach could hold. Following chemotherapy treatments, debilitating nausea was always a problem for her. I ran errands, did things around the house, and sometimes we just talked or sat quietly together.

My patient talked openly and without fear about her illness. The woman knew what she wanted, and chose to live as meaningfully as she could. Her attitude was beautiful, and it made me seriously look at my own life and how I wanted to live it. I followed her to her death. The experience was deeply moving, and it helped to clarify the subtle shifts in focus that were developing in me. The spiritual nature of our relationship in the last months of her life, filled me with a desire to become a chaplain, specifically a chaplain to the dying. When I look back at my journey and how terrified I was of death and people who were dying, I find God's grace simply amazing. The hospice experience showed me that I no longer feared death; rather, I wanted to work more closely with those who were moving toward it.

I had been at the Christian Life Center for nearly three years and knew it was time to move on, to take a risk, despite my anxiety of whether or not I would fail. There were no chaplaincy programs in Maine that fit what I was looking for, so I needed to look beyond the area. I was ready to branch out of the diocese, or out of the state, to get a different exposure. My Provincial gave her support, and in March of '91, I applied to Interfaith Health Care Ministries in Providence, Rhode Island. I was interviewed and accepted into its nine-month intern program which ran from September '91 to May of '92.

The Sisters of Mercy had a very large convent and residential home just outside of Providence, within easy travel distance to Health Care Ministries. The building was enormous and could easily house over 100 people. The sisters often accepted Interfaith students as boarders and fortunately I became one of them. I had a room, ate meals and attended Mass there, but I was basically on my own and came and went as I wished. It was a good arrangement because in addition to being a fulltime student, I often traveled to Winslow for weekend community meetings, and once a month, met with four other sisters with whom I'd formed community.

The group was made up of three very serious "thinkers," one "feeler," myself, and one sister who was a combination of both traits. We were friends, committed to religious life, and yearned to create something new that would make a difference. We met regularly, once a month, to share our life from various ministries and to grapple with the question of where religious life was heading. We wanted to form something that would be life giving, energizing, and at the same time, called us to our heart and soul. God was central to our purpose and we fortified and nourished each other's spirituality through acceptance, love, and prayer. We were asked, "What are you going to call yourselves?" We searched for a name to identify what we struggled with, what we were all about. We decided on the name "Chaos Community" because, within the larger community, we felt we were in chaos. "Chaos" provided a space in which to question old familiar securities, the meaning of life, and the authentic sources of human identity. Periodically, it came right down to examining our own uncomfortable feelings, and conflicts we had with each other or within our respective ministries. When sisters first heard about our name choice of Chaos Community, a little furrow would form between their brows, or their lips would tighten and the corners of their mouth would go down and they'd ask, "What are they up to?" They felt something mysterious was brewing because there were a number of strong people in the group. The truth was that we were trying to find our way, just like everyone else. Many sisters carried a vision, a few could articulate and speak for the community at large, but we were all confused as to how to make the vision real in concrete terms. This was our challenge and our mission. Meeting with this handful of sisters once a month was a cherished comfort and a support for me as I moved through the rigors of my pastoral internship.

The Interfaith program was an extremely busy and intense experience. There were classes and seminars in Clinical Pastoral Education that included health care issues, pastoral care training, and an in-depth exploration and processing of anger, stress, and other emotional issues. Three days a week we visited patients at a nearby hospital, and on Tuesdays and Thursdays we met for classes, supervision and group discussions. During supervision, we reviewed our interaction with patients through written reports called verbatims. The verbatim included the patient's age, gender, marital status, religious preference, date of admission, and the admitting diagnosis. We indicated the date, time, and length of visit, a detailed plan or goals for the visit, and observations made at the time. The actual verbatim traced the dialogue between the patient and intern from beginning to end. Part of our presentation included a personal evaluation of ourselves, and the pastoral opportunity our visit offered. We stated the facts as they occurred, our interpretation of what happened, and our reaction to the experience.

The supervisors were very hard on us, and at times, quite unnerving. We learned a great deal about ourselves, our strengths and weaknesses, and how we could integrate suggestions for improving our interaction with patients. Other chaplains and peers listened and challenged our approach to the patient. The confrontations were tough, and a part of me dreaded them. I knew it was helpful and necessary to develop pastoral skills, but that didn't make it any easier to digest. Rejection was a major issue with me, and it really came out during this training.

Tuesdays and Thursdays always ended with a group discussion. There were seven in our group. We sat in a circle, and it was up to us to further the meeting with our discussion. Supervisors were there to observe but not participate. The first minute or two were the worst for me. I do not do well with silence, a lifelong trait that was soon recognized by the group. We had a frustrating little routine going. My peers knowingly smiled at each other, and then one or the other would say, "Just sit here a few minutes and Linda will get us going." Sure enough, I'd start to feel uncomfortable and then I'd begin talking. I nearly always started the group. There were times when I was quiet because someone else needed to take the lead, but it was always grueling to sit with the silence in group settings. It didn't take me long to feel at home in the quietness of a patient's space; however, that wasn't the case in the beginning.

My first day at the hospital was memorable. My assignment was to visit patients, but I wasn't sure what I was supposed to do or say. I walked into my first patient's room, introduced myself, and offered to spend a little time with him to see how he was doing. He totally ignored me. The second patient told me in no uncertain terms that he could care less that I was there. I said, "Okay," and left quickly. My third patient was an older lady who was sitting in a chair when I walked in. As I approached her, I began talking and again, no response. The woman's roommate said, "She's deaf." She hadn't heard me, so I felt relieved. It meant I wasn't a total failure, but nothing worked out that day the way I imagined it would.

My expectations of patients and myself were unrealistic. I wanted to enter a patient's room and have them welcome me and like me. If they didn't, I thought sure I was doing something wrong and blamed myself for not doing it right the first time. During group discussion with my peers, I was forced to look at and address my issues of abandonment and rejection. My difficulties arose with certain patients, with critiques from my supervisors, and confrontations with peers. My reaction to an unresponsive patient prompted supervisors to ask, "Is it important that everyone likes you? Remember, you're walking into someone else's space and these people are not well. It's not about you, it's about them and where they're at." More than once I needed to reflect on a patient's feedback until I slowly learned that it wasn't personal. For a while, though, it was rough going.

Incorrect assumptions were another recurring theme. I remember walking into a room, where the patient was sitting in her chair, and there was a suitcase on her bed. I sat down, told her who I was, and in the midst of the conversation I said, "And you're going home today." She said she was. I added, "You must be so happy." She said, "No, I'm not." She wasn't happy because she was going home alone and was afraid to be by herself. This admission opened up an opportunity for her to talk about her feelings and to receive some emotional support which she very much needed. It was a beginning. Maybe I could do this, after all.

Another time I was with a woman who had just learned her cancer was inoperable. She was extremely sad and distressed that her little five-year old girl would grow up without her mother. The thought that she would not be there for her was unbearable. The situation was heartbreaking. A part of me was deeply shaken by this woman's story. I had just left her room when I was told that the person in the next room was very ill and was asked if I would go and visit that patient. I gave myself a minute to catch my breath and entered the room. The patient was in bed sleeping and three adult sons were present. While speaking with the sons, I said, "This must be really hard to watch your dad's sickness." They said, "Yes, it's very difficult to watch our mother." I almost died! The woman had very short hair pushed back and masculine features. I made myself go over to her and prayed to hide my embarrassment; however, the sons appreciated my praying with their mother. The next day, on a return visit, I was a little more relaxed. The sons were happy to see me and never commented about my blunder. As an intern, I was again reminded, that it is important to know exactly who was in the room before going in. We couldn't assume that whomever sent us to a patient would think of telling us everything we needed to know.

Early in my training when I met a patient who was not interested in talking with me, I wanted to run out of the room. After I learned to be more comfortable with myself, I was able to say, "I understand. It's okay. I just wanted to say hello and see how you are. If there's anything I can do, I want you to know I'm here." Other times I would say, "It really sounds like you've been hurt, and if at anytime you want to talk about that, please feel free." Sometimes the patients picked up on the invitation and talked about what they were going through. They'd say, "I've been really hurt by the Church, and I don't want to have anything to do with it." I'd respond by saying, "It sounds like you've been carrying this hurt for quite a while." I spent time listening to them talk about the pain they had been holding, or the divorce they had been through, or how church members had said something that affected them for most of their lives. Many were dying and felt God would not forgive them. I would ask them to forgive themselves and to trust that God had already forgiven them. Some let me know how much my acceptance of their thoughts and feelings meant to them. The imminence of death is always profoundly intimate and real. For those who can talk about their experience, the ego and personality seem to easily fall by the wayside. I cherished these soulful moments with patients.

Sometimes, what I encountered in a patients' attitudes was a startling reflection of behavioral patterns in my own life. The need to stay strong and be in control, at all costs, was a habit that I was all too familiar with. Mrs. "S" taught me how to let go of that a little.

When I first visited Mrs. Saunders in her room, she was lying in bed with her head elevated, watching TV. She was a large woman of 64, had short brown hair with grey highlights, and brown eyes. She looked rather pensive and forlorn, but greeted me warmly and entered into conversation immediately. After I introduced myself, she turned off the TV, and invited me to sit down next to her.

Her face was round and swollen, and a large scar from a surgical procedure covered the left side of her face. Her jaw had been resectioned and reconstructed due to cancer. Her mouth was still sensitive from the surgery and speaking was difficult, but it was clear she had a need to talk. I asked how things were going for her.

"I came back into the hospital on Sunday," she told me, "because I have an infection in my mouth. I'll be here until they can get rid of it. I really didn't want to return to the hospital quite this soon!"

"Oh? What happened?" I asked.

"I was in here a little over a month and a half ago. I had cancer in my jaw. They had to reconstruct my whole jaw." By now, talking was difficult and she had to speak slowly through clenched teeth. "I've been through so much in the last few months," she continued, "but the doctor told me they were able to remove all the cancer cells."

She raised her hand and touched her jaw saying, "Doesn't look too pretty, does it? But you know, Linda, in time this scar will mend and heal. I am just so grateful to God for more time, more time to live, but it hasn't been easy." At this point her eyes begin to fill. My heart was aching for her, and I reached over and touched her hands. I said, "Mrs. Saunders, sounds like you've been through some really difficult moments."

She immediately responded, "Oh, I have! I keep telling myself I have to keep fighting. I promised myself I wasn't going to give up, no matter what! I knew God would give me the strength I would need. I keep telling myself, I have to be strong."

When I inquired about her need to be strong, she explained, "My husband died just about a year ago, and I knew I had to be strong. If not, I might just give up, and I didn't want to give up!" Mrs. Saunders began to cry, I reached over, took her hand, and said, "It's okay." I just sat there stroking her hand while she cried.

I said very little after that because words suddenly became unimportant. Just being with her, touching her, and letting her cry was enough. Mrs. Saunders did not have to hold her pain by herself, and she did not have to be strong or in control. She could allow herself to feel all that had been trapped inside of her for months. I felt I was touching more than her hand, I was touching the holy space she was in at that moment. Allowing another to be, allowing another to speak, and not interfering with the release of tears and pain, was to me an encounter with something very holy. I felt touched by grace to be with Mrs. Saunders in her experience.

After a few moments, she looked at me with tears in her eyes and said, "Thank you, Linda." I sensed she was tired from talking, and when I asked, she just nodded. We said our goodbyes, and I told her I would see her the next day. She smiled slightly as I left the room.

I learned that day that when we allow ourselves to be held in moments of weakness and pain, we can then allow ourselves to move through that weakness into a real strength of soul that reveals who we really are beneath the need for control. On that day, Mrs. Saunders allowed me to really see her, and I loved what I saw.

Throughout the intern program, I had excellent teachers and supervisors, people who were really grounded in their own personal experience and faith, and who knew firsthand what they were teaching. But, the real facilitators of my spiritual growth as a chaplain were the patients themselves. More often than not, their experience, and the way they lived it, propelled me to my knees. So many brought a clarified view of life, facing the reality of their illnesses, and expressing how difficult it was when loved ones remained in denial. My first visit with Mrs. Lovely. was a perfect example.

Mrs. L was lying in her bed with her head slightly raised when I walked in. She was wearing a hospital gown and a blue and white satin bathrobe. She had blue eyes and a very soft, gentle look about her. Her blue turban highlighted her eyes and attractively covered her hair loss due to chemotherapy. Her room had many signs of love and affection. Cards and flowers filled her side table and a large get-well helium balloon gently danced on the ceiling above her bed.

Mrs. Lovely greeted me warmly when I entered, and she soon entered into conversation with me about her condition. I asked how she was doing, and with a touch of sadness, she replied, "Not too good. I'm rather discouraged today. The treatment they gave me didn't work. I have cancer, ovarian cancer, and now there's nothing further they can do for me." I was listening closely. She continued, "I've had cancer now for two years, two really hard years in my life! Two years ago, I wasn't feeling good, and I went to the doctors. I had all kinds of tests and they found NOTHING!" Her emphasis on nothing was strong and carried feelings of anger and helplessness that went right through me.

"Time and time again," she said, "I went to the doctors and still they found absolutely nothing wrong with me. I couldn't stand it any longer. Finally, one doctor advised exploratory surgery. I went through the surgery and only then was I told I had ovarian cancer."

"Ovarian cancer," I said, "Mrs. Lovely, that must have been really hard news to hear!" Tears welled up in her eyes. "My family just cannot deal with the fact that I have cancer," she said, and after a slight pause added softly, "and neither can I. When you're young, you think you're going to live forever. At 62, I still consider myself young. I have a wonderful family and beautiful grandchildren, and I want to see them grow up. This is just not fair."

Her voice trailed off a little and I asked, "It's not fair?" She looked at me and continued. "I keep telling myself that I have to keep fighting. I'm not going to give up! I know God will give me the strength I need to keep going."

Of this she seemed certain, so I asked, "You believe it's God's strength that is keeping you going?" "Yes, oh yes!" she said. "Cancer is so hard to deal with. My faith and my belief in God has kept me hoping. I've always believed that God sends no more than a person can handle. Though right now," her face clouded over as she finished her thought, "I've had enough."

This was obviously a difficult admission on her part. I said, "This is a real tender time for you, Mrs. Lovely I hear your pain. You've had enough." She began to cry and whispered, "I have had enough. Thank you for hearing my words and for not making them holy."

"Holy?" I said.

"I use the word holy," she explained, "because so many of my friends want me to feel better, so they don't really listen to me. I don't need to hear pious platitudes. I just need someone who will listen and be with me. Excuse me for saying this, but damn this illness."

When she talked about pious platitudes used by others to deny her pain, my heart cried. "It's okay, Mrs. Lovely," I said, "it sounds like you have a flood of feelings to share." "Yes, yes I have," she said, "I'm really trying to be strong for my family, so I'm not talking about my own fear."

Just then a nurse came in to take Mrs. Lovely's blood pressure. Mrs. Lovely turned to me and thanked me for stopping by and asked if I would come again. I assured her I would.

My encounter with Mrs. Lovely evoked many feelings within me. I was especially moved when she spoke about her inability to share her pain and fear with family and friends. I could have been talking to myself. As I left her room, I knew something had happened to me. I wanted to listen and be with her, but not to take away her pain or minimize her story. Sickness is not pretty. To witness others facing impending death, to see them grapple with fear and unresolved issues is not easy. If we can enter into their journey, we enter into the sacred mystery of life and death, and how unconditional love ties the two together. Mrs. Lovely blessed my life because she allowed me to live her mystery with her.

Overall, it was not an easy year for people in my group. It was agonizing to explore with supervisors and peers our intimate feelings and emotions — how we choose or don't choose, what we avoid, deny, or don't want to look at. An issue that was particularly difficult for me to confront was anger. I didn't think I had any. I did know that I couldn't risk ever being angry with someone because they'd abandon me for sure. A cheerful, lighthearted person is not supposed to get angry. It doesn't fit the image of a nun or of the giving person I thought I was. Through group discussion, I began to see how much anger and how many "shoulds" and "should nots" I carried within me. Working with the very ill and the dying inevitably moved everyone toward greater self-awareness and honesty. Memories returned: the deaths and losses within my family, the 15-year old patient in the nursing home of long ago, my own mortality.

My peers confronted my anger openly, and out it came. It showed up when I cried, otherwise I wasn't aware of it. I was angry with the fact that I wasn't in touch with my own anger. I couldn't believe how it revealed itself in my tears, my body language, my words. The truth of my anger was humiliating to the core. I was angry with my father for abandoning us and very angry with my mother for leaving me. People who didn't like me, or I thought might not like me, made me irritable. Patients made me angry when they didn't accept me. I got angry at my peers when they disagreed with or challenged the way I handled a patient, and I really became defensive when supervisors criticized me. My body would tighten up, and what made me the angriest, they'd immediately inform me of my response. My friend Kevin, a fellow intern, would say, "Get real, Linda." They'd also say my verbatims were, as others had described me before, "pretty."

I struggled with insecurity my whole life. Whatever I'd write, people would say, "Yeah, so?" or "That's nice. What are you saying?" I worked so hard at explaining myself, but people, and now my peers, would say it's not real. I'd think, well, to hell with you. This is me. I worked as hard as I possibly could to explain myself, and you don't get it. Then I'd cry, and I'd realize how angry I really was. Little by little, my supervisors and peers kept chipping away at me. I was like a rock that they chiseled over and over. Finally, something happened. Interfaith brought me to an inner reality where I was less than perfect but much more human.

I confronted my powerlessness and realized there was nothing I could do to stop death from happening. It forced me to look at how I wanted to live my life because every day is a small death. As I went through this evolution, the topic of my religious vocation would sometimes come up and subtly unnerve me. I had no words, just a feeling that maybe something was not right, but I denied the experience. This was an unconscious decision. For the moment, it was a barely audible, a small, unhappy voice. It was several more years before I could really listen and tolerate the message of that small voice.

I completed my internship in May and took advanced training from June through the first week of August. My specialized area was oncology and death. The two-month program required an ongoing peer review plus an intensive review before a group of supervisors. The review occurred midway through the program. We were challenged to see if we could really handle death and dying. The supervisory review turned out to be the most devastating experience I had ever gone through. I went in thinking I was in charge; I knew what I was doing, and felt I was in control of myself and what I had learned. My meeting was in July right around the time of my brother Bobby's anniversary.

The meeting moved along. The supervisors asked me different questions, and I was confident in my answers. In the course of the discussion, I happened to mention Bobby's death, and one supervisor, George, asked me how I was feeling about that. I said, "I'm okay. I'm feeling fine." George looked directly at me and said, "You're full of shit." I said, "Full of shit???" He said, "You're full of shit. I want to know how you're feeling." When he said that, it was as if he saw right through me, and it exposed a tender wound. I said I was okay, but he had put his finger right on my denial, and my real feelings surfaced like an eruption from the inner most part of my being.

I started to cry, more than cry, I was sobbing and I couldn't stop. George asked again, "I want to know how you're feeling." It took a few minutes to regain enough composure so I could talk. I said, "This is very difficult. I'm sad. It's a very sad time, and it brings back a lot of memories. Death is hard; loss is hard, and I'm feeling empty." I started sobbing again and had by then polished off a box of Kleenex. I looked around and some of the supervisors were crying. At one point George handed me his handkerchief, and I took it.

Eventually, the end came and there were no more questions. George said, "Linda, you can leave, we're going to discuss you now." And then he added, "Can I have my handkerchief back?" I said, "No." He said, "Could I have my handkerchief back?" I said, "I'll wash it and make sure you get it back." George came back with, "Give me that handkerchief." I felt I needed to be in control, so I said, "I'm not going to give you this wet thing. I'll take care of it, and I'll give it to you later." He wasn't about to back down either and said, "Give it to me." The tears started all over again. I gave George his handkerchief, left the room, and went into the restroom to pull myself together.

I came out and sat with my friend, Barbara, who was there with me to await their decision. She had her arm around me the whole time I waited because I was still so distressed and close to tears. They eventually called me back in and told me I had passed. George said if the interview had not happened the way it did, they would not have allowed me to go for my advanced training because, "life is not like that, and you need to be honest with yourself and admit where you're at." I was crying the whole time they were talking to me, I had no control. I left there sobbing and couldn't believe what had just happened. I actually passed! That same day, I also learned I had a job.

∞

TEN
PASTORAL CARE

In September, I joined the pastoral care team at Saint Anne's Hospital in Fall River, Massachusetts. When I was offered the position, I knew I'd be in the area for a period of time, and with permission from my Provincial, decided to get my own apartment. I had never lived alone before, but there was a growing need for my own space and the privacy to evaluate what I was living. I needed some solitary time with myself and with God, and the flexibility to receive people and to orchestrate an already hectic schedule. With help from my friend, Barbara, I found a small apartment in Tiverton, Rhode Island, that overlooked a river and was a reasonable commute to Saint Anne's. By August, I completed my training and returned to Winslow to settle my affairs before starting my new job as chaplain. I met with the Provincial Team. Because it was so out of character for me, they expressed concern about my living alone, but blessed my decision which was important to me, and told me I would always have an office at the Christian Life Center. I packed my things, and then scrambled to find pieces of furniture.

That same weekend, the sisters congregated at our Provincialate to elect seven delegates to attend the community's international General Chapter scheduled for France in January 1993. At that time, the General Superior and members of her Team are elected for a six-year term. In Maine, monthly work meetings had been held all year to discuss the community-at-large, and to hammer out three themes our Province would present at the international Chapter. The themes chosen were earth, woman, and the impoverished. These were then worked into the demographics, employment statistics, and resources of Maine. We put together a slide presentation and created a service ritualizing the themes that had become sacred to us. We also needed to elect a contingent of seven representatives to the General Chapter.

I learned that my name was among several other nominees on the delegate ballot. We voted for one delegate at a time. A two-thirds majority vote was required to win. The voting took some time, but it was moving right along until the last delegate position, for which I had been nominated, had to be decided. Then, the tension began. Ballots were collected, names read aloud and counted, but it was too close. We had to vote again. Other delegates got in on the first vote which meant they had the full support of the sisters. Inside I was dying. Thoughts raced through my mind and collided creating anger, fear and shame. What's happening here? They don't want me to go. I really don't fit in after all. Without the community's support I'm not sure I wanted to go. I held my breath. The second round of votes was counted and read aloud. I had hated these out-loud votes — they always seemed to be too personal. This vote was still inconclusive. The vote was too close, and we had to vote again. Inside, distress rippled through me like fingernails on a chalkboard. God, I prayed, please let me out of here! This was an ego nightmare for which there was no waking. The irony of this scene was that it would have been much easier not to go to Chapter. I had a profound desire to give my all to make religious life work for me and for others. I wanted to make a difference, but it wasn't necessary to go to France to do that. I would have preferred eliminating my nomination altogether, but all I could do was sit there and wait until it was over.

Poised at the third countdown, looking out the window, I noticed streaks of yellow-rose from the setting sun. The elections should have ended an hour ago. The final tally was in. This time, I received the required majority vote. I think the sisters were tired of voting. Someone turned to me and said, "It was really hard because I wanted both of you to go." Another was less tactful. She said, "I felt we needed to have an older person because we already have some younger people going." Naively, I really thought that most people voted on the merits of a person and how well she matched the position. Inside, a part of me felt cut adrift. I left Winslow that evening for the five-hour drive to Tiverton. The car was jampacked, but I cleared a little space on the passenger side for a box of Kleenex. I either cried, sobbed, or teared all the way back to Rhode Island. I was so grateful to drive up to my apartment that night.

Until January, I returned once a month with the other delegates to the Provincialate to finalize our yearlong preparation for Chapter. Each time, a new part of me did not feel at home in Winslow, but I soon became so busy and thrilled with my new job that at first I hardly noticed.

At that time, Fall River was a struggling mill city with high unemployment. Many of its 100,000 residents originally immigrated from the Azores, a group of islands off the coast of Portugal. As I got to know my way around, I marveled at the diversity of people and how I ended up working in the same city where my father grew up. Saint Anne's is a small, acute, care hospital in the middle of the city operated by the Dominican Sisters of the Presentation. Four of us made up the pastoral care team. In addition to our services, we also coordinated different program areas that involved an ever increasing number of volunteers.

Among the pastoral staff were Sister Carole, the director; Father Michael, Chaplain, and Sisters Marie Therese, Lorna, and myself. I was assigned to the oncology unit and clinic on South 3, and periodically was on call throughout the hospital. Different kinds of acute care situations made our work very intense. Being part of a team was crucial. We were in partnership with and for the patients, and I loved it. Through pastoral care, we offered patients and their families support in the midst of their pain and suffering. Our commitment was to extend a sensitive awareness and presence to each one. We focused on the needs of the whole person: emotional, personal, and spiritual, including the silent yet powerful language of gestures and unspoken words. We were also available to the nursing staff and doctors because they, too, were dealing with incredible sadness and encountered death every day.

People of all ages were coming into the hospital with a disease that took away part of their identity as they had known it. It was as if the roots of their lifestyle, their way of being, were suddenly shattered by cancer or some other terminal illness. Sometimes, at the end of the day, my heart ached from the human dramas I had witnessed; however, interacting and working with members of the team and hospital staff was a constantly renewing and energizing experience. We became very close and bonded around the care of our patients and their families. We encouraged and supported one another as we moved with patients along their journey, and became really present to their experience. Harry was a powerful influence in this regard.

Harry was dying of lung cancer. He had fought the good fight, had gone through every avenue of treatment available, but nothing had stopped the cancer from progressing throughout his body. He was extremely thin, fragile, and at this point, bedridden. One night, Harry was alone and having great difficulty breathing. I went in, sat by his bedside, and quietly held his hand. Harry looked at me, and with some effort said, "Linda, I've lived my life, and I want to die." He paused to catch his breath and then added, "Can you help me die?"

I looked at Harry. I just held his hand, and with tears in my eyes I said, "No, Harry, I can't help you to die." He squeezed my hand and whispered, "Linda, just be with me." There it was, in one fleeting moment, Harry put it all together with such beautiful simplicity, "just be with me." It's not important what people say or do, only that they be present with their whole being. Harry died peacefully a few days later, but he profoundly touched my life with those simple words, words that often came back to me.

There were many others at Saint Anne's who showed me something of life through their suffering and their love. Some of them, such as Teddy, became friends whom I got to know very well. Teddy was flat on his back and hooked up to a ventilator for two years. Every day, his wife came to sit by him. They were always happy to see each other and were thankful for yet another week, or month together.

They loved being together, holding hands, smiling, just celebrating their time with one another. As a couple, they lived what love is, how love unfolds, and the beauty and magic that years of commitment and dedication fosters in one another. Theirs was an exquisite love story that touched everyone who came to know them.

On South 3, it seemed as if each patient was a unique story of sacred human drama. Both young and old struggled so valiantly against cancer. Some were able to walk out of the oncology unit in remission, while others came daily to receive chemotherapy and radiation. When on call, I was available to the whole hospital, including the emergency room, where I witnessed deaths by suicide, crib deaths, massive heart attacks, and a host of victims taken by tragic accidents. At such times, one needed to be present to family members and friends, and to the death drama that touched their lives.

The ending of a life is always such a profound event. Even if we know it is coming, the loss itself still feels tragic and unexpected. At Saint Anne's, I lived on the edge of a new reality for me, a new understanding that inevitably comes when interacting with death and dying. What is the meaning of life? What purpose do I have in community? How am I fitting in? Do I fit in? These were not new questions, but since the August elections, they followed me like silent companions whenever I went to Winslow for chapter meetings. Instead of getting simpler, religious life became more complicated for me. I, not the community, was responsible for my state. The problem was I didn't know where to go from where I was. Within myself, I was struggling to make religious life work for me. A part of me wanted to be a savior and do something to make the community flourish. I wanted to make a difference. I believed religious life was intended to call forth the Spirit in each one and to be faith affirming in every way.

At the end of January, I found myself walking the beach off the coast of Locquirec, France. It was a beautiful site for the Congregation's two-week International General Chapter. I was by myself, picking up shells, and praying aloud, "Oh, God, help me. God, please help me. I feel so empty." My thoughts were muddled, so much so, I barely talked clearly. I went through the motions at meetings and plenary sessions, but I was distracted and overwhelmed with the emotional pain of separateness we were experiencing in our Maine delegation.

Since the "infamous" August elections, the delegates periodically challenged one another with differences of opinion as to how things should be articulated or presented. The conflict occurred when too many of us resisted change or another's point of view, especially while we were in France. Interpersonally, we all seemed to pull in different directions. It was as if some of us were allergic to one another. I prayed for an antidote or some kind of non-allergenic reprieve, but it never came.

Someone referred to our dynamics as "spiritual growing pains," but personally I thought we were just expecting too much.

In contrast, our sisters from the provinces of Mexico and India were doing very well. Vocations were up and missions were expanding and flourishing. Their cohesiveness, camaraderie and outright love of life were beautiful to see. I wondered if that's what awaited us in Winslow once we outgrew our growing pains.

Flying back to the States, I thought of the congregation and how much I loved the sisters and our committed lifestyle of mission. Chapter was incredibly difficult and confusing, but I saw it as an opportunity to renew my dedication to make religious life work. I believed the words of our outgoing General Superior in her opening message. "Along with all Christians," she said, "we are called to be prophets — to be prophetic demands depth transformation — change of heart, change of attitudes, change of lifestyle, change of whatever keeps our focus on ourselves, on our settled ways. It is not easy to accept a move to "elsewhere," wherever the Spirit leads. It certainly involves suffering and continual conversion." Little did I know how dramatic the Spirit's "elsewhere" would be for me two years hence. For now though, I was really happy to return to work at Saint Anne's. My life in Fall River was far from perfect, but among hospital colleagues, I found a daily supply of encouragement and support, and I needed that.

After my return from France I worked briefly with Betty, a 56-year old woman who had been in and out of the hospital and was failing rapidly due to lung cancer. One evening I was on call, and around 2:00 a.m. I was paged to return to the hospital. Betty had taken a turn for the worse, and her children asked if I would come in. When I arrived, her seven adult children were surrounding her bed. I walked over, told her I was there and that we were going to say a prayer with and for her. I invited the family to gather and hold hands as I offered a spontaneous prayer. I asked God to watch over Betty during this sacred time in her life, and to give her children courage as they watched this moment with their mother. Invoking the prayer taught by Jesus, I invited them to join hands with their mom as we prayed the "Our Father." The atmosphere became reverent, peaceful, and as we neared the end of the "Our Father," Betty opened her eyes real wide, gently closed them and took her last breath.

The children were distressed and found their mother's "sudden" death difficult. After the initial shock, I invited each of them to remember the good times with their Mom and what she had individually blessed them with. This was an opportunity to say goodbye, to bless her, and to ask her for the strength they needed. One by one they came over to Betty, made the sign of the cross, kissed her cheek, or brushed her forehead, and asked her blessings. Each one was visibly moved and felt he or she was both giving to and receiving something very special from her. These were holy moments that the family would always carry with them.

I walked this journey so often with patients. We often live as if our lives will continue indefinitely, and the inevitability of death is far removed from our thinking. The possibility that everything can change in an instant, that life as we know it can end, remains for someone else, but not us; however, when the threat is real, when there are no longer any options left for physical healing, a terrible aloneness can descend. Within that aloneness, the failures in one's life, in relationships with others and with God, become intensely magnified. In general, people have very little experience of being loved for who they are, myself included. It's very difficult for us to believe that we are precious in our Maker's eyes. I witnessed this over and over with patients who were approaching death. It is this "dying" need for unconditional love that shaped and molded my understanding of a person's final moments.

I took it upon myself to do my best to assure that no patient I was with should die feeling he or she had failed in life. It was helpful for them to recognize that we all make blunders, and we all fall and that we're all here to comfort, support, and help one another. I shared the God of my youth who was so much bigger than the Catholic Church, its laws, and its judgments. "God loves us as we are," I'd say, "and He does not hold anything against us. God knows we make mistakes, and it is through those mistakes that we grow and become the person we are."

There were times when patients were nearing the end, and though they had not been part of the Church for years, I intuited they still had a desire to receive the Eucharist. In my heart, I knew the rightness of being responsive to a dying person's desire for the host. To Catholics, receiving the Eucharist is the focal point of their spiritual life. Jesus would never deny anyone the gift of His Body and Love, and neither would I. I would simply ask if they wanted to receive.

Sometimes they would answer, "No, I can't." I'd say, "I'm not asking if you can, I'm asking if you want to." Some refused, but others would say, "Oh God, yes!" Together we'd ask God's forgiveness and that He'd hold this moment as precious. I would take the Eucharist in my hand, raise it slightly, and say, "This is the Lamb of God who takes away the sins of the world. Happy are those who are called to this supper," and we would spend a few moments praying together. I offered the Eucharist, saying, "The Body of Christ, my friend." For some this was a significant moment of peace, comfort, and, in some cases, unexpected reconciliation. They breathed their last with what seemed to be an acceptance of self and of God which felt holy and sacred to me.

Months passed and my involvement and responsibilities in Pastoral Care extended into educational areas which I really enjoyed. Sr. Carole and I coordinated days of recollection in the greater Fall River area for eucharistic ministers. They were reverent times of prayer, reflection, and spiritual renewal. We worked with deacons who ministered at the hospital, giving them a two-week evening series on the impact of pastoral care. I became involved with the National Cancer Foundation and gave various lectures on the topic of "Caring and Spirituality." I presented a workshop on "Spirituality" to a group of nurses, psychologists, and social workers. There was no question that interest in matters of spirituality, especially with death and dying, was growing among health care professionals.

In November of '93 I began a patient support group called *Footsteps*. We explored the difficult emotions, experiences and spiritual issues connected with having cancer. The group had a slow beginning, but I continued to meet regularly with whomever would come, even if it were only one person. Word about the group got around, and little by little our numbers grew until there were about 10 regular members. It was rare, however, that all 10 would come the same week because of chemotherapy, radiation, or generally, because some were not feeling well. Some had lung cancer, others leukemia, but the vast majority of women had metastasized breast cancer. The group evolved into a safe haven where intense feelings were shared with others who were in the same situation. The women developed a camaraderie, a real union and communion with each other. They shared their lives, gave mutual support, love, tears, and their own special brand of humor. Journeying with these women was a gift and privilege.

My sense of compassion was increasingly shaped by being with patients and their families in their encounter with death. For families especially, the emotional sides of their lives became unleashed, sometimes spilling over into anger, remorse, and fear. Sometimes they experienced guilt for grieving while the loved one was still alive. Healing on some level was only possible by allowing them to express whatever they were feeling and being present to their pain. This was hard. It took me a long time to realize they had to deal with their own anger, that it wasn't my job nor could I take their anger away. In the beginning I wanted to fix it, to make it right because they asked me to. I thought I had to have the answers. I didn't.

So often, I walked into a room where someone had just lost a loved one and that person would come at me with his or her overflowing feelings. With a kind of wild sadness in their eyes, they would say to me, "I hate God," or, "Why is God doing this to me?" or, "How can God, who is supposed to love us, allow this to happen;" to take away my child; take away my mom, my dad, or my husband? I'd stand there and let them say what they needed. Afterward I'd say, "I don't understand either, and I don't know why this is happening, but I can be here with you." Somehow, we would get through the moment without trying to sanctify the experience, or make God a God of love when they weren't feeling that way or even considering it.

Ministering was allowing patients to be where they needed to be, at the time they needed to be there, while not trying to change their feelings. When working with people who were grieving, I often used what I had once heard at a conference — the three H's: hang around, hug, and hush. Hanging around was a sense of presence and being there for the other; hug was the ability to touch when someone needed to be touched; and hush was not being compelled to talk but being totally attentive and quiet with them. When people were grieving, they often needed to be quiet to experience the feelings they had. Presence was key with people who were hurting, simply touching them, holding their hand, holding the silence with them. I observed that people experienced love and compassion more powerfully with silent presence than words could ever convey.

At night when I left the hospital, I thought of my own life, what I wanted to live and what I was actually living. I felt called to live as a Sister of St. Joseph, a life that I loved, but in my heart was an unanswered question. I avoided the question because I really didn't want to face it, nor did I know how. Regardless of what I could or couldn't do, I could no longer deny the emptiness within myself. Each encounter I had with death called me further and further into my own heart that longed to be heard and listened to with the same openness and acceptance I gave to my patients. The lifelong pattern of giving to others while ignoring myself and my own needs had evolved into a chronic blind spot that I was as yet unable to see.

As each morning came, I returned to work, continued my life as a Sister of St. Joseph, and lived my commitment as fully as possible. I loved and honored my community, and cherished the thread of grace that wove my years of dedication and service to its way of life. All that I lived in community helped to mold, fashion, and cultivate God's presence in my being, for which I will always be grateful. The community had been a midwife to my spiritual birth and then had lovingly and compassionately nurtured my growth into a soulful core from which I could now evolve. Maybe, just maybe, that is why unforeseen events suddenly catapulted me into my hidden self which I so desperately wanted to avoid and deny. Maybe, I now had enough inner strength or resiliency to tolerate seeing what was really inside of me and what might be calling me to something else.

ELEVEN
TWO PATHS

The New Year of 1994 came and went. It had been two months since I'd settled into a new apartment in Fall River. It was a little smaller than the one in Tiverton, but it was closer to work, and it came with a washer and dryer, very prized commodities. Being on my own, yet attached to the community, was a wonderful experience. I'd learned to stretch in hundreds of little practical ways related to earning a living, running a household, and building on the lifestyle of service I had developed with the Sisters of St. Joseph. Gradually over the past 10 years, I'd felt the community needed to move forward and out of the province of Maine. My heart, too, carried both an inner and outer need for personal expansion. Since the Interfaith training in Rhode Island, building on my California experience, I had felt the same outward movement that I wanted for the community.

I very much loved my job with Pastoral Care. I was busy and often worked beyond the end of my shift. It was difficult for me to walk away from a new patient or someone in need just because my workday officially ended. Sometimes it was the only time I'd had to call a few patients at home to see how they were doing. Some were recuperating from surgery, while others like Debbie, were weathering the ordeal of chemotherapy or radiation treatments. Despite several surgeries and nearly continuous chemotherapy for two years, the cancer had slowly progressed through her body.

I first met Debbie Pestana in February of `93 when she was

111

admitted for hip surgery to replace bone loss due to metastasized breast cancer. It was an early evening visit. I walked into the room. There were no lights on, and Debbie's curtain was drawn. I pulled the curtain aside and found her lying on her back with her eyes closed. I bent over to be in her range of vision and, speaking softly, introduced myself. I didn't know if she was sleeping, but she opened her eyes. "Debbie," I said, "my name is Sister Linda. I'm a chaplain here and I just wanted to come by to introduce myself and see how you're doing." She didn't respond but continued looking at me. I talked for just a little while and asked if she would like to receive Communion. She said, "Yes." I whispered a short prayer, gave her Communion, blessed her, then smiled and said "Goodnight, Debbie." A couple of days later I was on my way to France for the General Chapter and was away for two weeks.

For some reason, Debbie needed to be with me, and whenever she came to the hospital, she inquired as to my whereabouts. Usually I knew which patients I'd see that day. I worked from a roster of South 3 in-house patients and outpatient appointments for chemotherapy or radiation. I didn't realize at the time how important my visits were to Debbie, or how much our interaction dramatically changed her attitude, at least during our time together. We visited one day for about an hour while she was on the drip end of intravenous chemotherapy. As I left her room, Debbie's husband, Louie, caught up with me in the hall and asked, "Do you make house calls?" I didn't know what to say because I had never been asked that before. Louie continued, "You do for my wife what no doctor, no medicine, no psychiatrist could even think of doing. I don't know what it is, but you guys have bonded, and it's mind-boggling to me. When you're around Debbie, she behaves as if she weren't sick at all. Sister Linda, I will pay you for your time to come to the house if you can." I said, "That's not necessary. Just give me your phone number and address, and I will call from time to time."

And I did call. Louie would say, "I can't get her out of bed. She doesn't want to get up. The shades are pulled low, and she just wants to lie there." I'd say, "Let me talk to her." Debbie would get on the phone, and we talked, joked a little, and I'd ask her if she wanted some company. Debbie would say yes, and I told her I'd be there in an hour. Later, Louie told me, "As soon as Debbie got off the phone with you, she'd say to me, "Louie, give me my wig, get me an outfit and get me my shoes. Sister Linda's coming over." She'd get out of bed, fix herself up, and sit on the couch so eager to see you. You two would laugh and visit for a couple of hours and my wife acted as if she wasn't sick a day in her life. Then you'd leave and Debbie would go back to bed and not want to get up again. Sister Linda, there's definitely signs of progress when you're with her."

Like some patients I'd worked with, Debbie never acknowledged or talked about death and dying. The fear and repression were so strong that it prevented others, including Louie, their teenage daughter, Jennifer, and Debbie's parents from addressing the obvious and the inevitable. The intensity of Debbie's denial, over which she had no control, was emotionally painful and paralyzing for everyone. As chaplain, the rule of thumb was simple: take patients as they are, and go where they're at. Acceptance, presence, and compassion — tender medicine for an aching, terrified heart. The painful drama of Debbie's illness eventually brought us together in friendship, and in a way I could not have ever foreseen.

In early spring, the Provincial asked me to give serious thought about being Formation Director for the community. Nomination ballots had been sent throughout the community, and my name was one that had been submitted. Another sister and I talked about a new cooperative venture or team approach to Formation. The team format would combine the vocation and formation director positions into a shared co-position. Through meetings, prayer groups, and retreats, we'd work with women who were considering religious life and accompany them through the discernment process. Once someone decided to enter the community, we would journey with and mentor that woman in her religious development through to first vows. As a team, we'd work closely with the Provincial Team in developing the shape and substance of the new formation concept.

Current formation was in three stages: first was the Affiliate program. During this phase a woman continued to live in her present environment. The vocation director guided the affiliate with recommended readings, retreats, workshops, and visits to local communities. After a period of time, mutual consideration, and if the woman expressed interest in joining, she was accepted into the Associate program. The status of the associate was one of candidacy. She was not yet a member, but by living in a local community she was able to experience the congregation. She continued her professional work, was expected to be self-supporting, and she shared in community functions and responsibilities for the house. The third phase involved a two-year novitiate training in preparation for first vows. This formation period intensified the new member's experience of shared faith with others. Her life was balanced between solitude and prayer, and community life and ministry. The novice had the opportunity to study and assess the nature of religious life, and the mission and spirituality of the Sisters of St. Joseph.

The thinking at the time was that I had completed my chaplaincy training, and the other sister was returning from a sabbatical year which allowed her to easily move to Fall River. She and I could then initiate planning stages for the team approach. The possibility that the program would be taken out of Maine into Massachusetts was being addressed by the Provincial Team. Unlike young parochial school recruits of the past, we knew we would attract women of different ages and backgrounds. Our doors would be opened to divorced women, older women with grown children, women in their 40s and 50s who wanted a second, more spiritually grounded lifestyle, or maybe even women who wanted a temporary time with the community. In my view, we needed to look beyond where we'd been and how we previously had done things.

Whenever the community had asked something of me, my immediate inclination for the past 24 years had always been in the affirmative. If the community had a need, and I could fill it, there was no question I would try. It was an automatic reflex. Very quickly I envisioned this house of prayer and discernment to be one of hospitality and enthusiasm. Our life had to show a vitality, something of excitement for people to wonder what we were all about. In the heart of our commitment, we needed to capture this aspect of hope, of mutual support and aliveness for religious life which I sometimes felt was lacking. I was in a time of discernment for myself without really being aware of it. What I was aware of was a vague longing for things to be different. We were capable of being different if we just worked at it hard enough and long enough. Some people in community just didn't seem all that happy or excited about religious life. Television programs, such as, Jeopardy and Wheel of Fortune provided a shared evening experience for some, while others preferred to knit or crochet together. I loved these sisters, but my sense of community seemed increasingly different from theirs. I couldn't see how these activities would carry the necessary energy to attract vocations. I believed we needed something different.

Formation Director was an important responsibility, and I was well aware how challenging it could be. The position held respect, but it was not exactly a coveted or popular position. Sisters were not waiting with bated breath for this nomination. Several key sisters whose last position was formation had left the community. The discernment of one's own calling, as well as others, often became challenged or clarified through this particular placement. Later, discernment for me took on a whole new dimension that I never would have dreamed of. Unfortunately, at the same time, all of my hidden agendas and unconscious masks spontaneously became undone. It would be six months, however, before I became fully aware of it.

Work at the hospital that spring was incredibly busy. The pastoral team was going every minute. We never lacked for patients, and we had more training groups coming in for workshops and seminars. The chaplaincy was immersed in me, and I in it. Over and over, we walked the last mile, the last days, the last moments of people's lives, and with each, we walked this intimate road with their family as well. One didn't have to be a chaplain to breathe-in the holiness. It was just there, like a soft holy gift for anyone whose heart was open to it. No matter how often one experienced the death of another person, it still shook the tendrils of one's life. It was always the same, yet it always felt new, like a birth. Holy is holy, and gradually I felt myself changing inwardly.

During this time, I saw Debbie Pestana only once in a while when she came in for treatments. In between treatments she, Louie, and sometimes Jennifer took vacation trips together. One day Debbie told me, "Louie is always ready to book a trip for us. Wherever I want to go, he makes sure I get there. He says he wants to give me something to look forward to. Sometimes the trips are a little difficult, but we do manage to have fun together." Debbie always brought something back for me from her trips. Personally, and as a member of the pastoral staff, we didn't encourage gifts, nor were we supposed to accept presents, but Debbie needed to do this. It was her way of saying "thank you," or "I care about you." Giving little gifts or souvenirs was her language.

Debbie showed her appreciation by giving things, never with words. She could talk about her nails, her clothes, but she never touched the reality of what was happening to her, and that's where I'd naturally go. That's where I felt at home, but you couldn't get there with Debbie. I wanted her to come to peace with her dying, but not everyone wants to respond in that way, or even respond at all. I didn't spend a lot of time with her, but when I did, it was challenging. I'd talk and she'd listen. She'd respond to questions but the conversation had to be pulled out of her most of the time. I was glad for both of us that I could speak, and that Debbie, more importantly, wanted and needed to hear me. Keeping in touch with her was important because she needed me, and the only way I could bond with her was through prayer and the Eucharist. She always wanted Communion and to be blessed and prayed with. She was like a young child who was completely overwhelmed with what was happening to her, and no one could stop it from happening.

I had known the Pestanas for about a year when, during the spring of `94, an event happened that drew me closer to Debbie and her family. Simultaneously, but in a different part of my life, I was involved in serious, sometimes heated, discussions about formation. These two profound experiences ran side by side, never touching one another. Before the end of the year, both dramatic journeys unfolded in natural progression, yet never intersected. Some people believed otherwise, which is what people sometimes do when they don't know the full story.

I was at the hospital the day Debbie's legs gave way in the parking lot. Louie had driven her to the hospital for her scheduled radiation treatment. He helped her get out of the van when they both realized she couldn't stand up; her legs buckled underneath her. Louie couldn't hold on without hurting her, so he laid Debbie gently on the ground. A man walking through the parking lot came running over.

"Get some help," Louie told him, "go inside and get some help." In less than a minute, hospital staff ran out and placed a board under Debbie. They picked her up, put her on a stretcher, and carried her into the hospital. Debbie had two hip replacements. The reason she couldn't stand was because the cancer had spread to the remaining bone in her first hip replacement. Dr. Shparber, Debbie's oncologist for the past two years, took Louie aside and said, "Louie, I think it's out of control. I'm going to have to do a little more investigating, but it doesn't look very good."

In the meantime I was called and met Louie outside of Debbie's room after his talk with Dr. Shparber. His eyes were wide, he was barely breathing, and he was unsteady on his feet. In halting words, Louie told me what the doctor had said and then he fell apart. He was sobbing and kept repeating, "The cancer's spreading, the cancer's spreading." It broke my heart to see this grown man cry, to see how much he loved his wife, and how helpless he felt to protect her from the disease. Then, like so often before, he pulled himself together and went to call their daughter, Jennifer, and Debbie's parents. His job was to hold the family together. There was something about this incident that touched deeper layers of compassion and insight in me. A muted sense of hopelessness permeated the family, compounded by the denial that Debbie's body was in the final process of dying. No one could talk about it, but everyone was living it. When spring moved into summer, Debbie's cancer leveled and became a little more manageable. It was a needed calm before the storm.

My monthly interactions with Chaos Community began to intensify over my nomination for the formation team. They knew I could do a good job, but they were also aware that in taking the position, I would not be able to invest as much of myself in the group as I had. The configuration of our "community within a community" would change, and so would the aspirations that had emerged over the past couple of years. The whole situation was awkward, acutely sensitive, and seriously heightened conflicts in a revealing sort of way.

The five of us were a close-knit group. There was something very special about each one and about all of us together. I loved and supported these women, and more than anything, I wanted to work spiritually side by side with them. We had long thought of, and talked about, living something meaningful within our little community. Initially, I wanted to think this way, but I became increasingly less accommodating as I branched out on my own. I felt we were dividing ourselves from the larger community, which wasn't what I wanted to do. I felt divided within myself. Nothing was clear. I wanted to live a dynamic spiritual life with these five people, but not at the expense of the larger community. Taking the formation position was a way of bringing everyone together, somehow creating an easier path from the old to the new. I knew what I wanted to do, but I had a hard time giving voice to it. It was difficult putting words to my hopes and my feelings.

When I came before the Chaos group, I was in discernment and wanted their help in thinking it through. Secretly, I wanted their full support. I wanted them to give me their unconditional love, but that's not what happened. "You know," I said to them, "I think I'm going to accept this because I feel there's something I can offer. I really feel I can make a difference." A few kept asking, "What's the difference?" After the third time, I got flustered, "I don't know what that difference is! I'm not exactly sure how I can make a difference, but that doesn't stop me from trying. I know we need to change and maybe this is something I can offer." One shook her head. "Look," she said, "neither you nor anyone else is going to change the system. If you try to change it, you'll get caught in it." "Not necessarily," I said. They were convinced that change was impossible, and I was convinced otherwise. I certainly wanted to give it a try.

Our dreams and ideas for religious life were well spoken in Chaos, but we never did anything concrete with those ideas. It was not for lack of desire. There was tremendous desire and good intent, but what eluded us was the next step. We weren't clear on how we were to get there, so we just kept talking. With formation, I felt I could do something; however, it was painful not having their support. A part of me understood their position, but another part, the part closest to my heart, felt once again, cut adrift. I was beginning to feel lost, and sensed troubling winds were about to carry me to places I had never considered.

Back in Fall River, the other nominee for the new, joint, formation position, and myself, continued to meet and to negotiate different formation plans. Here, too, we had differences of opinion, and issues became increasingly more complex. We both preferred to be in a supportive role with formation and not the director. Neither one of us really wanted to take the responsibility, but someone had to take charge in order to get things moving. With each passing day, I became a little more frantic. I had a vague feeling that something was unraveling inside, but true to form, I plunged ahead. I found what I thought was a great rental house for the community which would meet all our formation needs. Unfortunately, the owner needed an answer within a week. I got on the phone and really tried to present my case to the Provincial. All I could envision was this beautiful, simple house and all the wonderful programs we could do there. All the Provincial could hear was an anxious, forceful, and nervous sister totally focused on getting the community to make this significant decision instantly. In retrospect, I was indeed somewhat heavy-handed, but at the time, I thought I was just being persuasive. After reviewing the information, the Provincial Team wisely decided it was too fast and too soon. In my emotional state though, I saw the team's decision as yet another instance of lack of support for me. The ground beneath my feet was beginning to crack, and all I could do was keep running to the next option I had, which was to look for a larger apartment for the other sister and myself. My formation partner was temporarily staying in Winslow, and my self-imposed pressure was continuing to build, and right about this time, Debbie began to fail.

It was late August, and the Pestanas had taken me out for dinner. Although she didn't eat very much, on the surface Debbie seemed to be doing pretty well; however, I could tell that she was losing ground. It was right after this meeting that she started to show signs that the end was approaching. Hospice was called in the following week, and within 24 hours all services were in place. I visited Debbie more often, bringing her Communion nearly every other day. We talked that first week when she was still coherent. Similar to six months before, she gave her second, and last, rare moment of communication. "Linda," she said, "promise me something. Promise me that you'll take care of my mom and dad, Jennifer and Louie." I said, "I'll be here to do whatever I can do, Debbie." She looked at me, took a breath, and said, "Be there for them." There was something in her words, and in the way she said them, that echoed inside me.

A few days later Debbie was no longer eating, barely talked and was slipping further. Two nights before she died, she lay quietly in bed. Jennifer and Louie sat with her, and Debbie's mother was in the living room. Suddenly, Debbie screamed out in pain and frantically stretched and reached for her legs. No one knew what was wrong or what she wanted. She mumbled between her screams, but no one understood what she asked for. There was a lot of commotion in the room, emotions ran high. She was frustrated with everyone and very much in pain. Louie moved in and began massaging her legs which calmed her until he stopped, and then the screaming and excruciating pain rose once more. Liquid morphine, prescribed for every 2 hours, was given at 10 to 15 minute intervals. For days, Debbie could barely move or talk. Now, she was sitting up in bed, reaching for her legs and mumbling between her screams. Louie was beside himself. He finally said, "Deb, what do you want? Tell me what you want." This time, she stopped, and very clearly said, "I don't want to die." With tears in his eyes, Louie held Debbie's hand and said, "You know, you've fought the fight and now it's time to take care of you, Deb. I'm going to take care of Jennifer, I'll take care of your mother and father, and they'll take care of me. Do you hear me, you've got to take care of yourself." She nodded yes, lay back down and eventually went to sleep. She passed away two days later, on Saturday evening, September 10th. Louie later told me that Dee, a close friend who was also an excellent nurse, offered to stay with Debbie during this time. This meant a lot to him. Dee was always present for the whole family, and it was she who confirmed Debbie's death. She said it happened right after Debbie heard that I'd called from Maine to see how she was doing. I drove down that night. Friends and family were still at the Pestana house, but Debbie's body had been taken away. As is often the case, Louie, Jennifer, and Debbie's parents were functioning but in a dazed, pained state. Even when we know death is imminent, the finality delivers a shock of its own.

The following day, I prepared a prayer service for Debbie. The house was once more filled with family and friends. People cried, and I cried with them. The heart is always moved with death and changed in very profound ways. I was working and on call the day of the funeral, and because of my beeper, I sat at the back of the church with another cancer patient who had been very close to Debbie. I left immediately for the hospital after the service. Driving back, I thought of Debbie and her silent, painful struggle with cancer in the 20 months I'd known her. As with other patients, I'd encouraged Debbie to make each moment count. In the midst of dying, I supported her choosing life. I reflected on my own life, and a strange feeling wafted through my body as I drove into the hospital parking lot. I had this strong image of Humpty Dumpty falling, smashing into many pieces, and being unable ever to put himself back together again. The wall I had so carefully built, brick by brick, over the past 25 years was about to come down, and I with it. All it would take would be one, small, innocuous shove.

TWELVE
THE CHOICE

We'd been in deliberations about formation for a good five or six months, and my fellow nominee's indecisiveness was increasing day by day. I had certain reservations myself, so between the two of us, formation plans moved at a snail's pace. I didn't want to leave my job, nor could I work fulltime and take primary leadership for the program. The realization also occurred that I was lost without support from the key persons in my life, and without that, something in me crumbled. People had been telling me that I was an ideal person for the formation team, but in reality, no one else wanted the job, not even my colleague. For nearly 30 years, the process of renewal had torn up the organizational fabric of religious life, and we still didn't have a viable plan of what to put in its place. Chaos Community provided new and exciting ideas and visions, but they were without a plan to make them real. The larger community offered security and stability, but remained inflexible and unyielding in the face of necessary, life-affirming changes. Again, I felt pulled in two directions and seemed to be imprisoned in a chronic dilemma. My fellow nominee and I were in fragile territory, both of us in need and both evolving, like two peas in a pod. The whole drama forced a deeply buried issue within me to surface, whether I liked it or not, and whether I was ready for it or not.

That September, after the Provincial Team decided against the house, formation was put on hold for the time being. My colleague and I agreed to give ourselves time to live together, form community, and see what would come out of it. There would be no pressure, no commitment. My small apartment couldn't accommodate both of us, so we looked for a larger place. We found a decent place in a good location, signed the lease, and gave a non-refundable $100 deposit. The next day, the sister, for various reasons, changed her mind about living there. We were $100 poorer and back to square one! I could have said, "Okay, let's check out something else," but instead, something in me screamed. I was pushed to the edge of my own effort at trying. To myself, I thought this is awful. I can't do this. I can't do this anymore. The community voted me in, but I'm not getting any support from the people I most need it from.

There was a large part of me that felt victimized by everything, and I didn't understand why I was unraveling. I felt broken. I had been trying for 25 years to fit in. I helped whenever and however I could, and now everything was held back. I felt that the support was not there. It all became magnified in my mind. In my room, I thought aloud, "I've had it with everything and everybody. I don't want formation, and what's more, I am not even sure I want religious life." My hand covered my mouth in shame. Oh, my God, I'd said it! I never wanted to say or think this. I'd always fought against the feeling by trying to fit into religious life. I never wanted to leave, and here I was thinking of leaving. A parade of questions marched through my mind. What's going to happen to me? Where am I going to go? What am I going to do? How will I support myself? I couldn't answer any of these questions. I only knew I couldn't do it anymore. I was reaching the end, getting closer and closer to making the hardest choice of my life. In my heart I knew I would leave. The when and how were what terrified me.

By the end of September, things had been set in motion over which I had no control. At home, I cried and anguished over what to do. In the morning, I put on my cheerful, bubbly self for work and dispensed encouragement and positive strokes to others throughout the day. I was busy with patients, various meetings, including my bi-weekly cancer support group, and *Footsteps*. After Debbie's funeral, Louie returned to the group for a while. The women loved it and were so happy to see him. He wanted them to know they weren't forgotten, and that he was there to support them. After everything he'd been through, Louie also needed support, and I suspected he received it by being there. It was about this time that Louie took me to the cemetery so I could see Debbie's grave. Louie needed to return, and I think he preferred not to be alone. Being there was terribly hard for him, and he began to cry. Instinctively, I walked over and put my arm around him for comfort, but something happened inside of me the moment we touched. I had feelings for him — feelings that a woman can have for a man. Oh, God, where is this coming from? It scared the hell out of me, and I did not want to deal with it. My life was already too confusing and terrifying without adding this! It was too much, just plain too much. Plus, I had already reasoned, when the time came to leave community, I wanted to leave this place and go where I wasn't so well known.

My formation partner returned to Maine the first weekend of October. Before she left, we talked at length. I told her of my confusion. I said, "Sometimes I don't know if we in community really love one another. We seem to have such a hard time supporting one another or being happy about our successes. I feel so much more alive here in Fall River working at the hospital than I do back in Winslow."

She understood what I was saying. I continued, "I don't know where I am right now. My whole life is being turned around here. I have all these feelings. I feel in crisis about religious life. I also have feelings of being attracted to someone, and I don't know where it's all coming from." This part got her attention. She asked, "Does the other person know?" I said, "No, he doesn't know, and it could be that my feelings will pass." She added, "I think you should get some counseling about all of this." I totally agreed. I knew I needed help. I also knew she was hurting and needed to figure out where she was with all that had happened over the past six months. I said, "When you go back this weekend, talk to whomever you need to talk to, do what you need to do for yourself. If you need to, let them know about me. If you can't come back here, don't feel you have to because I am struggling."

I don't know what I was thinking, but for some reason I thought she'd come back. I figured she'd be with me and not leave me alone in my struggle; however, neither one of us was in a position to help the other, and after much deliberation, she decided to stay in Maine. She came back for her things and left Fall River for good. This was it, my moment of truth. I was all alone. I didn't feel attached to the community. I didn't fit and didn't think I could live it any more.

Very quickly, I became introspective and the need to look at my commitment emerged with tremendous force. I'd look at it this way and that way, tried every angle I could think of, but it was useless. I was terrified to even think about leaving religious life, but I could no longer ignore the fact that the possibility was there and had been for a very long time. Humpty Dumpty was in my thoughts again. I felt broken, in pieces, and scattered. The model of being a perfect religious, and the importance of that in my life, literally fell off the wall. The Sister Linda, CSJ, image fell and shattered, and I couldn't put her back together again.

In my aloneness, I cried and cried, but most of the image of myself was gone. I had lost the ideal, the fantasy of the kind of religious I thought I was. The pain was unbearable. I'd pull myself together to go to work, then come home and fall apart all over again. When off duty and alone, I cried most of the time. I was losing weight and my eyes were puffy. I didn't have the benefit of makeup, so I hid behind a perpetual toothy grin. It was so contrived; it was pathetic. I was dying inside, but in front of others, I smiled as if everything were wonderful. I just couldn't let anyone at work or in the community really see the terrible mess I was in. That small part of my image still left, wouldn't allow it. This was a lifelong compulsion — show only what was good and perfect. It had done a good job supporting my image in the past. It would take a long while before I realized it was useless now.

I shared these experiences with my spiritual director, who strongly recommended I seek counseling, and a close friend referred me to a psychologist. I needed to get to the bottom of this and was relieved to get help with it. I only saw the psychologist three or four times, but that first visit is etched in my memory. He asked a little bit about myself, where I was coming from and what was going on. I couldn't talk without crying, but I managed to force a few things out. "I'm in a vocation crisis," I said. "I'm really struggling. I think I need to leave, but I'm not clear why I can't, or if I should leave religious life. It's been sitting inside of me for a number of years which I've been able to ignore until recently." I told him about formation and how it brought this truth to the surface. I described how I had always worked hard to be the best Sister of St. Joseph, and how that constant trying and continuous effort masked what was really going on inside. "I don't know what's happening," I said. "I think I need to leave. I'm not happy, and I feel I don't belong anymore. Maybe it's just a hard time now, and maybe I need to sit with it." I felt I had an entire lifetime of squelched feelings suddenly filling up and spilling over.

My first session ended, and another box of Kleenex was gone. The psychologist gave me homework I was not expecting. He put it this way: "Linda, I invite you to go home tonight and to sit quietly. When you feel ready, I want you to go into the basement of your heart and see what's there. I want you to look deeply within yourself and find what needs to be looked at." He warned me, "You're going to face a lot of things, so be prepared as you venture in. There's no return, Linda, there's no return. You need to go inside."

I left his office shaken by all that had come out of me, and then I thought, my God, I'm not very good at going inside. I didn't think anything would come out of my homework, but I was ready to try anything to get at the truth rumbling around inside of me. That night, I sat on my couch and decided I was ready to try. I pulled my feet up around my chest and hugged my legs. I closed my eyes, took several deep breaths, and allowed myself to unlock a door and step inside. I found myself walking down a long deep stairwell that was filled with all kinds of cobwebs. When I reached the bottom of the stairs, I saw a huge trunk at the end of the room. I edged my way over to it. There was a dark blanket covering the trunk on top of which was a thick layer of cobwebs. There was an amazing clarity to this experience. It felt so real and even the basement smelled dank and musty.

Anxiety rippled through me as I moved closer. I pulled one corner of the blanket and let it slowly slide to the floor, exposing an old, dark leather steamer trunk. Two voices in my mind loudly vied for my attention. One kept saying, "You've got to open this trunk. You've got to open it." The other voice was just as intent. "No, don't. Don't do it." The first continued, "You've got to open it." The second replied, "No, I can't." First one said, "Yes! Yes, you can. Do it now!" With a trembling hand, I gently lifted the lid and looked inside. It was dark, but tucked in all four corners of the trunk I saw fear, fear, fear, nothing but fear — my own fear. Oh, my God, I thought, is this what's been stopping me?

I stood before the trunk and realized what had happened. From my early years on the farm in South Berwick throughout my time in religious life, I had put every ounce of fear into that trunk. In each corner, I recognized not only my own fear, but a large dose of my mother's fears I'd absorbed since childhood. I'd taken in her tremendous anxiety of what other people would think and say and made it my own. It was now in my trunk and was my fear, all of it. The thought of leaving community was paralyzing, so the thought was never allowed. Unconsciously, I'd created an image of a perfect religious who always smiled, saw everything as wonderful, and never said no. The image of Sister Linda looked good, and she genuinely meant well, but when the trunk was opened, it showed that much of her was not real. She had to be perfect because that's what held the fear at bay. Only perfection would guarantee some semblance of acceptance, of fitting in. It was all there in front of me. I feared what other people would say, feared their rejection, and feared what was going to happen to me. I was terrified that leaving might not be the right decision, yet everything in me anguished at the thought of staying. I was imprisoned by fear and what it had done to me. As soon as I realized this, as soon as I realized I had a choice, a small light radiated from inside the trunk. Choice, it was about clear, authentic choice.

Left unchecked, fear had a power that robbed me not only of the moment but of my entire life. I was always afraid of what other people would think of me, of hurting someone, or of making a mistake. This was the story of my life. Accepting it involved making a clear decision to enter my own flesh and claim my past, instead of blaming it or escaping from it. It meant being true to my real feelings.

As I looked at the contents of my trunk, it made me cry. I became immersed with overwhelming grief for a lifetime of fear, fantasy, and false image. I cried for the unconsciousness of the past and the profound awakening of the present. I moved toward acceptance of my true being and the need to make a life change. It had been waiting for me for a very, very long time. I could no longer live as a Sister of St. Joseph, and once that decision was made, I felt a complete and joyful freedom. For the first time in my life; however, the sense of liberation was bittersweet, a mixture of joy and pain — pain for what I knew would lay ahead of me.

I met with the psychologist several more times to determine the best way to approach my departure. I continued with spiritual direction, and when I was clear in my own heart, I contacted my Provincial and asked to meet with her in person. She came down in October, and we talked for a very long time. I explained everything as clearly as I could, how taking a position of discernment had pushed me over the edge. Sooner or later, it would have happened. The truth of my image and its "fall from grace" was inevitable. Sharing this was very difficult, very painful, and we both cried. I needed to speak frankly and truthfully, and the Provincial really heard me. "Linda," she said, "I want to invite you to take a deep breath and plunge into the real work now of shaping your new possibilities. It's important for you to direct your energies toward a new life." Her acceptance and compassion covered and protected me like a blanket of mercy. My fear dissolved in our tears. In the end, she asked me to take more time to reflect and continue going for counseling, which I did, but the decision had come from my heart and seemed final. On the outside, it appeared very fast; on the inside, it clearly wasn't, and we both knew it. A few weeks later, I met with the Provincial again and told her I was definitely leaving. Fear is what was holding me, and I couldn't be bound to it anymore. Now, I had to prepare for the secular world.

I chose to leave, and part of me was still terrified to take the leap into the consequences of my decision. Identifying my trunk full of fear was only the beginning. The tentacles of that fear had deep roots, and each one needed to be extracted. It was hard. It was fire. It was hell. It was death, death to the image, kicking and screaming. For me the course was set, the train was moving, and I wouldn't be able to get off until it reached its final destination.

I continued working with oncology patients who were confronting life and death decisions all the time: whether or not to submit to a new chemotherapy series, or additional weeks of radiation, or any last niche of hope for a turnaround in the illness. I stood with them now and talked from a new place within myself that was similar to theirs. It was that fragile place of choosing or trying to choose the best path toward healing.

On my off hours, I spent a lot of time at home crying. I wasn't interested in food and was losing more weight. I felt I couldn't share with anyone at work what was happening for fear it would interfere with my ministry and work relationships. Increasingly, I despaired at trying to lead two lives, my muddled, fearful, personal journey, and my cheerful work persona. I had to notify a lot of people by phone about my decision. I didn't want to do it this way. I wanted it to be more personal, more one on one, but because I was working a lot of hours, that was not possible. I could only wish that they understood. I called my friends in Chaos Community and arranged to meet with them individually. I couldn't talk about this over the phone with them. The group was not happy and said, "No, don't do it. Linda, don't go." I said, "I have to do it. This is it. It's not something that happened overnight, though it seems as if it did." My family in South Berwick was totally supportive and offered to help in any way it could. Without hesitation, my family showered me with love and acceptance which made me realize how thankful I was for them; however, my decision to leave was very disappointing for the sisters in Maine. I know they felt betrayed because a few months before I'd said, "Yes, yes," to formation, and now I was leaving the community. They had no warning something was not right, because I had never let on, ever. Never letting people know there was anything wrong was such a big part of the image, and I cried a torrent of tears over what it had done in misleading others, unconscious as it was.

I had decided to leave my job at Saint Anne's and the area by the end of the year. I planned to stay with my family in Maine, and allow myself some time to think through the next move. I waited until December to tell the hospital staff and patients I was leaving, and I simply told them, I was moving back to Maine. Except for my co-workers and a few close friends, I was feeling too broken and vulnerable to tell people I was leaving my community. If people didn't understand, I wouldn't have been able to cope.

Had I to do it all over again, I don't know if I would have handled it differently. Right or wrong, I knew of no other way, given the limited stability I had. I did the best I could. I was so exposed, insecure and raw, I didn't think I could deal with the slightest insensitivity or misunderstanding. There was some unfortunate fallout, but ironically, not so much for leaving community. Some sisters, co-workers and others were convinced I left because I had fallen in love, a perception that really sharpened their tongues.

Around mid-November, Louie invited me to dinner with Jennifer and his in-laws. When the time came, everyone, except Louie and myself, begged off for various reasons. When he came to pick me up, I invited him into my apartment, which he'd never seen before. I wanted to share with him what had been happening. I'd known Louie for nearly two years, considered him a friend, and felt safe to talk with him. Surprisingly, it took all I had to tell him of my decision to leave religious life. With the community and my family in Maine, I was feeling increasingly isolated and really needed someone to talk to. It was then that I felt the depth of Louie's kindness and compassion. The man was not only supportive, but he really heard the pain in my voice as I described my journey. I felt, he saw and heard in a way I'd never before experienced. I was conscious of how short a time it had been since Debbie's passing, and prayed I wasn't burdening him with my problems. Out of nowhere, Louie asked, "You're not leaving for me, are you?" The question floored me, and I said, "Oh, no. No." Later, when he asked again, it occurred to me that maybe he had feelings for me too, which left me numb. We went to dinner. Both of us felt that something wonderful was happening. We talked a great deal and ate very little, but I felt ashamed. I'd just told this man I was leaving the community, and here I was eating dinner with him. It was overwhelming, and I was a mess. The next morning when he called to see how I fared with all the talking we did, my stomach felt awful, but I told him I felt wonderful, and I did.

December was a month for correspondence. The Provincial had written on my behalf and supplied me with all the information I needed for my dispensation.

There was no delay. I wrote to the mother house in France and sent them all my papers. I wrote a formal letter to the Pope requesting dispensation from my vows. I wrote to all the sisters in Maine, which was especially difficult. There is no painless way to leave any community. I was taking care of all of that, plus ending my position at Saint Anne's, saying my goodbyes as best as I could, and trying to work out where I was going after I'd leave the hospital.

In the meantime, my relationship with Louie continued to grow. Warmth, support, and presence were his constant gifts to me. He was my sounding board for the next step, for what I needed to think about, what I needed to be aware of. He really couldn't offer any advice, but he was there, present and aware of my journey. There were times when all I did was cry; that's all I could do. Everything about our relationship was secretive, therefore tense. I was still at the hospital, and officially, still part of the community. Even though I was leaving and papers were being processed, I didn't want anyone to get the wrong impression of a Sister of St. Joseph, or of me. I didn't dare go any place with Louie for fear of causing scandal. Ours was a blissful, happy courtship, but it was all but hidden from everyone.

On February 2nd, the official papal endorsement dispensing me from my vows arrived in Winslow. It was exactly 25 years to the day since I had entered community. When I arrived to sign the papers, I thought I would get very emotional, but I didn't. I was clear, and I was ready. Signing those papers was what I needed to do, and I was fine.

I had never known how important it was to listen to one's self, to one's truth. No one can teach another how to listen. It comes from that place in the heart that brings one peace. It's the same place where I ultimately found my God. For me, it was only through God's help that I was able to weather the year ahead of me.

PART FIVE
INTEGRATION

I believe the process of growth is the art of falling down,
falling down in order to pick oneself back up
with deeper knowledge and awareness,
an openness to continue taking the next unknown step
beyond the edge into self-discovery.
The basic truth remains that God is mystery.
It is from this faith that the heart speaks best.

THIRTEEN
THE TRANSITION

The hardest decision I ever made in my life was to leave religious life. It would have been so much easier, less emotionally shattering and difficult, to spend the rest of my days in community. To avoid where I'd emotionally been and what I was about to physically go through, would have been my choice in the past. The slightest sign of pain or discomfort, the lifelong penchant of denial with a wonderful smile was where I'd go. That strategy, unconscious as it was, wasn't working anymore. Over the past year, I'd learned that when the soul awakens, its painful journey of faith will not be denied, much to the chagrin of the body.

I spent the first three weeks of 1995 in a "transition fog" while packing up my belongings and terminating my residence in Fall River. There was a lot to attend to with the apartment and people in the area. I'd pushed my body emotionally and physically to the limit without being aware of what I was doing. Similar to my experiences in Auburn and then Winslow, I was out of touch with my body's distress signals, and now it had serious, mutinous inclinations. After I'd left Saint Anne's at the end of December, my body slowly began to deteriorate with one thing after another happening to me. I noticed a lower back pain, and I developed a urinary infection that seemed indefinitely resistant to medication. Later I had headaches, sore throats, and a terrible pain on my side that took my breath away. I'd been under stress the whole year, and now my body let me know it had been through hell and back.

At the end of January, my sister Cora and her husband David came to Fall River and helped me move to New Hampshire. They welcomed me into their home with open arms, and provided a wonderful space for me to rest and think things through. Their love and support comforted me during very difficult days. They, like the rest of my family, were outstanding in their acceptance, and gentleness with my healing.

The community was also very generous with me in my departure, which really touched my heart. From the onset of my leaving, the Provincial was remarkable in her compassion and kindness, and I will always love her for that. Her attitude and focus sculpted a new space for former religious like myself, that in our personal confrontation and choice of truth, we were no less a part of the lives of the sisters.

I'd always loved the community. A part of me was profoundly affected by the charisma of the community, a part that will always be a Sister of St. Joseph. The Provincial saw it, welcomed it, and blessed me in my new life. She understood this was not a divorce, but a necessary change in my soul's journey, that neither I, nor anyone else could alter.

The transition from religious to civilian life was at first very difficult. Without the image of Sister Linda, which had meant everything to me for 25 years, I felt vulnerable, and I feared the reactions of others. Physically, I was drained, but my spirit felt very alive as I adapted daily to the surety of my decision. Life was very different now, in that, I had the challenge to recreate my life into something brand new.

Louie's presence in my life was a real gift. I cherished this man who had a wonderful *joie-de-vivre* and a very infectious laugh, but it was really his character that I fell in love with. On so many occasions, I had witnessed his devotion to Debbie, his attentiveness to her needs, and his desire to make every moment of her life special and memorable. He treated his wife with honor and respect, which was very different from how I'd seen men behave when I was growing up.

His sensitivity, however, touched me the most. Louie had cried and shared with me the anguish and fears surrounding Debbie's illness and death. He was protective of his family, and it tortured him when he couldn't shield Debbie or them from the cancer. There is no question I felt safe with this man.

Our relationship, begun about two years before, grew from mutual respect and appreciation for who we were as persons. We had seen each other at our best and at our worst, had enormous respect for one another, and we had a solid history based on friendship and support. Though we were now very much in love with each other, we each still had to negotiate through some very difficult emotions. Louie still grieved for Debbie, and experienced ambivalent feelings for caring about me. He struggled with the guilt he felt when he presumed people would say, "It's too soon." I was grieving the loss of being a Sister for 25 years, and trying to balance a dramatic change in lifestyle. I was thrilled, but very confused with all my new emotions. Falling in love remained a real mystery to both of us, but we trusted God and the new path that was gradually being revealed to us. We knew our relationship was a good thing, a very good thing.

The most challenging experience Louie and I had was telling people, especially his family and friends, about our relationship. We didn't want to hurt anyone. We tried very hard to be sensitive with Mary and Sid (Debbie's parents). They had known me as the Sister Linda who had helped and befriended their daughter for the last two years of her life. We knew it would take time, patience, and understanding to receive their blessing and approval of us as a couple; however, the person we were most concerned about was his Louie's daughter, Jennifer.

Like Mary and Sid, Jennifer had known me as Sister Linda and as her mother's friend from Saint Anne's Hospital. Her father had already spoken to her about us, and some time later, so did I. I went over to the house to talk and spend time with her. I needed to express my thoughts and feelings directly to her. "Jennifer," I said, "I don't understand why all of this has happened, but it has. I want you to know that I care a great deal for you, and I love your dad very much, but I would walk away from this experience if it were going to hurt you or your relationship with your dad in any way. You are both too important to me. I need you to hear me say that."

Jennifer said, "Linda, I was a little surprised when dad first told me, but I'm okay now. I just needed a little time." I nodded and then added, "Jen, I'd never try to take your mom's place. The only thing I can do is be Linda for you, and I'll always be here for you. Do you hear me, Jen?" That was our beginning.

My first night out with Louie's brother, Fred, his wife, Carmen, and their friends was memorable. I was nervous, anxious, and eager to be accepted and loved as part of a couples' world. I was 46 years old and not at all accustomed to dating or "going out" with a group of men and women. They turned out to be simply wonderful people. Within a short time, I felt accepted and welcomed, and I gratefully noticed how happy they were for Louie and me. It meant a lot to both of us. After that evening, we began to tell others about our daily growing relationship. Many were happy for us; some were not, but we quickly learned to create a new life surrounded by people we loved and who loved and supported us.

Louie and I met on weekends. I needed the week in New Hampshire to reflect on what I was going through. I'd drive to Fall River on Friday for an appointment with my chiropractor, and then spend the weekend with Louie and Jennifer at their home in nearby Swansea. During the week, Louie and I talked on the phone at least once, sometimes twice a day. It got to a point where we wanted to be together so much, that I started making excuses to come down earlier on Friday, or sometimes Thursday mornings. Louie came to New Hampshire a couple of times, but I did most of the commuting.

It wasn't easy living out of a suitcase, surviving an aching back, and facing my own fearful projections. Every weekend, I'd have to battle the anxiety of what people would think about me staying in Louie's home. In my heart, I knew what I was doing, but the inner critic in my mind was still merciless. Despite our very kosher arrangement, with a daughter in the house, I continued to feel pangs of guilt. We had separate bedrooms, honored each other, and above all, Louie respected who I was.

News of my weekend jaunts traveled quickly throughout Saint Anne's, igniting some hurtful rumors. Some comments hurt and infuriated me, such as, I was a "real disgrace to my community." That one hurt me to the core, because I'd never have done anything to harm the community, nor was I doing anything wrong now. One doesn't do damage to a piece of one's soul. Like a broken refrain, I'd repeatedly say to Louie, "People who know me, will know me and know us, and people who don't, will make judgments, and there's no amount of talking that can change that."

We really supported each other through this time, because Louie was also getting hurtful reactions from some of his friends. We reminded each other, that overall, people were very supportive and happy for us. It was just a handful, that for reasons of their own, were very disapproving of our relationship.

I'd overheard Louie tell a friend, "I did everything I could for Debbie. I made sure she enjoyed life right up until the end, until there was nothing else I could do. I don't feel I did anything wrong by falling in love with Linda. She's a wonderful person. It wasn't preplanned, and I've nothing to hide. It just happened. It's not too soon for me to get on with my life, and maybe some day we'll all find out why things worked out the way they did." Like Louie, I, too, didn't know why he came into my life at the time he did, except he did, and it was one of the greatest gifts God could have bestowed upon me. It was a gift just knowing there was someone present to hold me, who was exceptionally sensitive and caring, and who accepted me unconditionally without question. I didn't know of a more beautiful gift one person could offer another.

By April, I knew my back wouldn't handle driving back and forth much longer. I had pain in my upper and lower back, had bladder problems, and was physically exhausted most of the time. Commuting was becoming too difficult. I toyed with the idea of getting an apartment near Louie's home or possibly staying with friends, when Louie invited me to stay with him and Jennifer. My anxiety level immediately shot up. I thought, my God, here I go again, wondering what people are going to say, or what they're going to think. I had to trust my heart and do what I needed to do. Louie and I both knew our love was real, there was no stopping it, and that we'd eventually marry. Late October seemed to be a respectful date for all of us. It was important to Louie, Jennifer, and myself that a year's time had elapsed since Debbie's passing, before making a formal commitment to one another. It was also very important for Debbie's parents. Our relationship was moving very fast for them, too.

Moving in with Louie and Jennifer required enormous adjustment for all of us. The house was very much Pestana. Everything that was there had a family link between Louie, Jennifer, and Debbie. I needed to give myself time to adjust and also time for them to adjust to my being in the house. Debbie loved cats and they were everywhere in the decor. There were cats all over the place: cat frames, cat pictures, cat trays, cat wall hangings and more. At first I was afraid to do anything, but I needed to feel I could fit into my new home.

In her quiet way, Jennifer was very accepting. I'm sure it wasn't easy for her. Her mother had been ill for nearly five years, had passed away less than a year ago, and all these changes of the past few months were being thrust upon her by the adults around her. I was very sensitive to her. Some days, it wasn't easy and I felt uncomfortable. Jennifer didn't talk very much, and I wasn't sure how she felt or thought about the situation. On the surface, she seemed happy with my presence, so gradually, I unpacked my things and began to let it become home for me.

Louie was terrific. He said, "Linda, this is going to be your home. You need to feel you're a part of it." He gave me free reign! The first thing I did was reorganize the cupboards in the kitchen and bathroom, and only after we were married did I make more visible changes throughout the house. The cats, I'm pleased to say, have been retired to storage for Jennifer, should she want them some day.

The pain in my back softened a bit once my commuting days were over; however, it never quite left me and by late May, the pain returned more intensely. One morning, I woke up to find that I couldn't bend to make my bed. I had to kneel, keep my back straight as a board, and make my way around the bed in that position. Louie was worried. I didn't want my back to be a problem for anyone and decided to just cope with the pain as best I could. My resolve weakened as the pain worsened.

By the end of June, I went to a doctor who thought I had arthritis; prescribed medication, and recommended I go for physical therapy. It sounded like a good plan, but two days into it, the pain worsened. Louie insisted I get a second opinion and have X-rays taken. While waiting to be seen, I stood in the waiting room with tears in my eyes, because I couldn't sit at all. I felt better standing up, but the pain made me very fidgety. The doctor saw us after viewing the X-rays and said, "I don't know who told you that you had osteoarthritis, but what you have is much more serious." I'll never forget his expression; he looked so somber. "It's one of two things," he said, "it's either a tumor or a disc problem." We just looked at him. Later, Louie said his body just went cold when he said that. The doctor added, "You've got to have an MRI. Go home, and I'm going to schedule one for tomorrow morning at 11 o'clock, and then we'll see where we're going."

That night I tossed and turned and got very little sleep. I relived the same scene over and over. I kept seeing the doctor's expression when he said, "This is serious..." If this is a tumor, maybe, I've had it for quite a while. Maybe, I'd waited too long. "This is serious," he said, and on and on. I decided that if there was anything terminally wrong with me, I was going to leave the relationship. I couldn't put Louie through another experience with cancer. I simply wouldn't do that to him and Jennifer and told him so. I was determined.

That evening, Louie took Jennifer aside and said to her, "Something's wrong with Linda. I don't know what it is, but we're going to find out. She's going for an MRI tomorrow morning." Jennifer asked, "Any idea what it might be?" He shook his head and said, "The doctor said it was one of two things, either a tumor or a ruptured disc or some kind of disc problem." Jennifer got upset and said, "Why is this happening to us?" Louie tried to reassure her that we didn't know what it was yet. "But Jen," he said, "whatever it is, we're going to be there for her. Linda told me she would walk out of our lives before she'd put us through anymore cancer. I told Linda she wasn't going anywhere, I wouldn't let her. You know, I don't have to be married to have a commitment." Jennifer said she felt the same way. Louie was clearly worried and said, "Jen, if it's a tumor, what are we going to do?" She said, "We're going to take care of her. There's nothing else we can do."

All I did the whole night was lie awake in a fetal position. I was in excruciating pain and couldn't put my legs down. As soon as I did, the pain would shoot right back up again. The next morning, Louie came into my room and said, "Linda, I'm taking you to the hospital." I said, "No, Louie. I'll be okay." As soon as I said that, I knew I wasn't. I can't do this to him, I thought, something's terribly wrong. The pain was just too bad. Louie persisted, "There's no way you're going to take the MRI this morning unless they ease your pain, and the only way they're going to do that is if you get to the hospital early and have a shot." I went along with him, because I didn't have the energy to argue. Louie tried to help me out of bed, but the pain made it impossible. He didn't waste any time calling 911. The ambulance drove to Saint Anne's Hospital, and they gave me medication as soon as I got there. It alleviated the pain enough so that I could at least get into the MRI cylinder.

The technician said to me, "Okay, Linda, you have to lie real still. You can't move any part of your body. It messes up the X-ray, and we'd have to take it all over again. This is going to take about 40 minutes. Try to relax and don't move, okay?" I nodded, but to myself I thought, my God, I'll never be able to do this. For the whole time I was in the MRI, I closed my eyes and said to myself, I can do it, I can do it, oh, dear God, be with me, I can do it. Louie had come in with me, stood at the end of the machine and held my ankle. I could feel his comfort and support. What I couldn't see was that he was looking up at the ceiling thinking that if there is a God, He wouldn't be doing this to him twice. Louie knew something was clearly wrong, didn't know what it was, but prayed his heart out that everything would be okay.

I came out of MRI, and we went back to the emergency room to wait. About 15 minutes later, the doctor came in and said, "Linda, looking at your X-ray, I see that you have a herniated disc, a ruptured disc that needs to be taken care of right away. This is bad." I cried out in relief, "Oh, no, it's not!" I had tears in my eyes, and I was smiling. I couldn't believe it. Both Louie and I were crying for joy that it wasn't a tumor. We knew it was fixable and surgery would take care of it. The next day I had an appointment with a surgeon in Providence, Rhode Island who concurred with the diagnosis after looking at the X-rays. He explained, "What's causing you so much pain is that the disc broke and chipped. A piece of the chip went down into your fifth vertebrae and it's pushing into your sciatic nerve. You must be in severe pain!" "Tell me about it," I said. He went on, "I don't perform surgery on anyone unless they really need it, but you need major surgery as soon as possible." I was scheduled a week later.

For a week, I lay flat in bed with my knees up into my chest. I was on strong medication that really knocked me out, but as it wore off, the pain became unbearable again. The medication raised havoc with my bowels, and when I'd get up to go to the bathroom, I couldn't sit because of the unbearable pain. The whole situation was very grim. I couldn't take any medication the day before the surgery, so by the time I reached the hospital my body was in terrible spasms of pain. I was told to wait because there were no gurneys ready for me. I couldn't stand; I couldn't sit; I couldn't lie; I was dying with pain. Louie saw what was happening, lost his patience and scolded the hospital staff, "Look," he said, "you've got to do something for this woman. She's in incredible pain!" They did. Within minutes they gave me medication that barely touched the pain, but it helped me to carry on. I knew that more than anything else, I wanted to get into that operating room.

The surgery went on as planned and when I came to, I was lying on my back in the recovery room without any pain. For the first time in years, I was without pain. Within a few hours, I was taken back to my room. I had been through some serious surgery, but I was hungry and relieved. I had an incision in my back, and I knew I needed to be careful, but I was so happy. The doctor came in and said, "You're incredible!" In my pain-free status, I was thrilled with the operation and his skill as a surgeon. He said, "I want you to know I did extensive surgery on your back. You really needed to have a lot of work done which means you'll probably be in the hospital for the next three days." Later, after he had examined me further, he decided to release me the next morning.

I went home and recuperated quickly. I believe that attitude had a lot to do with it. Every surgery is different and everyone experiences pain differently. The day I came home, I ventured outside for some walking exercise because the doctor strongly recommended it. Walking was the best thing I could do to facilitate healing. I was outside when some neighbors walked by. Louie told them I had just had back surgery. They looked at me in awe. They couldn't believe how well I looked and moved. At night however, I'd wake up with intense cramps in my legs, which I had been told to expect. I'd have to stretch the leg muscles and walk more every day, which I did. Within two weeks, I was doing great and feeling fine. I had to be careful, couldn't bend or lift, but I could move. As far as I was concerned, I had everything to live for. I was deeply in love with Louie, was profoundly loved by him, and we were getting married in three months, on October 28th. There was a lot to do, which added extra emphasis to getting well quickly.